PAT PAST PAPER WORKED SOLUTIONS

Copyright © 2021 *UniAdmissions*. All rights reserved.

Previous Editions: 2020, 2019, 2018

ISBN 978-1-913683-38-2

No part of this publication may be reproduced or transmitted in any form or by any means, electronic or mechanical, including photocopying, recording, or by any information retrieval system without prior written permission of the publisher. This publication may not be used in conjunction with or to support any commercial undertaking without the prior written permission of the publisher.

Published by *RAR Medical Services Limited*

www.uniadmissions.co.uk

info@uniadmissions.co.uk

Tel: 0208 068 0438

PAT is a registered trademark of Cambridge Assessment, which was not involved in the production of, and does not endorse, this book. The authors and publisher are not affiliated with PAT or Cambridge Assessment. The answers and explanations given in this book are purely the opinions of the authors rather than an official set of answers.

The information offered in this book is purely advisory and any advice given should be taken within this context. As such, the publishers and authors accept no liability whatsoever for the outcome of any applicant's PAT performance, the outcome of any university applications or for any other loss. Although every precaution has been taken in the preparation of this book, the publisher and author assume no responsibility for errors or omissions of any kind. Neither is any liability assumed for damages resulting from the use of information contained herein. This does not affect your statutory rights.

PAT PAST PAPER WORKED SOLUTIONS

SAMUEL PUTRA

ROHAN AGARWAL

ABOUT THE AUTHORS

Samuel has a DPhil in Engineering Science from Trinity College, University of Oxford. He obtained his MEng degree from Oxford with First-Class Honours, graduating in the top 4% of his class. Since his undergraduate years, Samuel has assisted many A level students with their university admissions, providing tuition for entrance exam preparation and guidance for interviews.

Samuel holds a teaching role as Graduate Teaching Assistant at Oxford, providing tutorials for undergraduates in Chemical Engineering Modules. His research is focused on Sustainable Wastewater Treatment and Energy Recovery which has secured several awards including Best Poster in Water Category at Concawe Symposium 2017. In his spare time, Samuel enjoys going to the gym and playing football.

Rohan is the **Director of Operations** at *UniAdmissions* and is responsible for its technical and commercial arms. He graduated from Gonville and Caius College, Cambridge and is a fully qualified doctor. Over the last five years, he has tutored hundreds of successful Oxbridge and Medical applicants. He has also authored ten books on admissions tests and interviews.

Rohan has taught physiology to undergraduates and interviewed medical school applicants for Cambridge. He has published research on bone physiology and writes education articles for the Independent and Huffington Post. In his spare time, Rohan enjoys playing the piano and table tennis.

Contents

The Basics 6
2006 10
2007 27
2008 46
2009 66
2010 88
2011 109
2012 130
2013 153
2014 172
2015 195
2016 215
2017 237
2018 255
2019 276

PAT PAST PAPER SOLUTIONS | **BASICS**

THE BASICS

What are PAT Past Papers?

Hundreds of students take the PAT exam each year. These exam papers are then released online to help future students prepare for the exam.

Where can I get PAT Past Papers?

This book does not include PAT past paper questions because it would be over 1,000 pages long if it did! However, all PAT past papers since 2006 are available for free from the official PAT website. To save you the hassle of downloading lots of files, we've put them all into one easy-to-access folder for you at <u>https://www.uniadmissions.co.uk/every-past-papers-answer-sheets/</u>.

How should I use PAT Past Papers?

PAT Past papers are one the best ways to prepare for the PAT. Careful use of them can dramatically boost your scores in a short period of time. The way you use them will depend on your learning style and how much time you have until the exam date but generally four to six weeks of focussed preparation is usually sufficient for most students.

PAT PAST PAPER SOLUTIONS BASICS

How should I prepare for the PAT?

Although this is a cliché, the best way to prepare for the exam is to start early – ideally by September at the latest. If you're organised, you can follow the schema below:

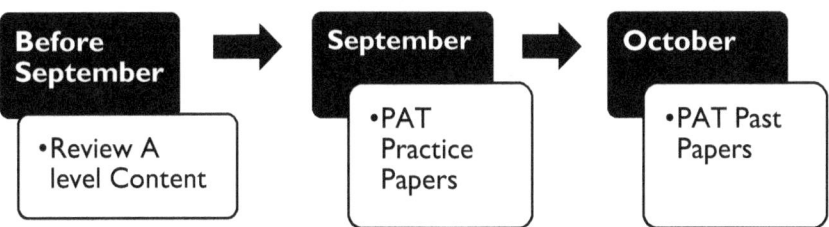

This paradigm allows you to minimise gaps in your knowledge before you start practicing with PAT style questions in a textbook. In general, aim to get a textbook that has lots of practice questions e.g. _PAT Practice Papers_ – this allows you to rapidly identify any weaknesses that you might have e.g. Newtonian mechanics, simultaneous equations etc.

Finally, it's then time to move on to past papers. The number of PAT papers you can do will depend on the time you have available, but you should try to do each paper at least once.

PAT PAST PAPER SOLUTIONS — BASICS

HOW SHOULD I USE THIS BOOK?

This book is designed to accelerate your learning from PAT past papers. Avoid the urge to have this book open alongside a past paper you're seeing for the first time. The PAT is difficult because of the intense time pressure it puts you under – the best way of replicating this is by doing past papers under strict exam conditions (no half measures!). Don't start out by doing past papers (see previous page) as this 'wastes' papers.

Once you've finished, take a break and then mark your answers. Then, review the questions that you got wrong followed by ones which you found tough/spent too much time on. This is the best way to learn and with practice, you should find yourself steadily improving. You should keep a track of your scores on the next page so you can track your progress.

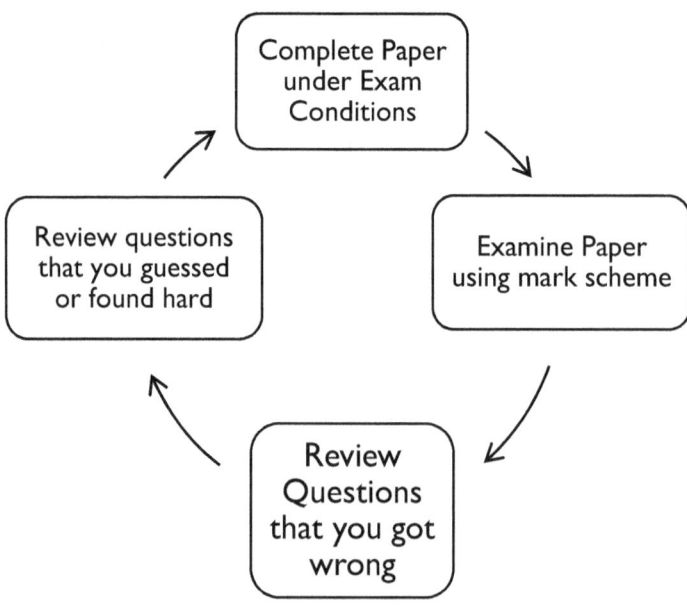

PAT PAST PAPER SOLUTIONS | BASICS

Scoring Tables

Use these to keep a record of your scores – you can then easily see which paper you should attempt next (always the one with the lowest score).

PAPER	1st Attempt	2nd Attempt	3rd Attempt
2006			
2007			
2008			
2009			
2010			
2011			
2012			
2013			
2014			
2015			
2016			
2017			
2018			
2019			

2006

PHYSICS

SECTION A

Question 1: C

The term u is initial velocity (m/s), whereas the term t is time in s. Hence ut is velocity × time which is **displacement** (m).

Question 2: A

First, we need to find the volume of the block: $V = 3 \times 4 \times 5 = 60 \text{ cm}^3$. Then, the mass of the block is given by

$$m = \rho V = 8570 \times 60 \times 10^{-6} = 0.5142 \text{ kg}$$

By definition, pressure is force/area and so the pressure will be maximised when the block rests on the face with the smallest area.

$$p = \frac{F}{A} = \frac{mg}{A}$$

$$p = \frac{0.5142 \times 10}{3 \times 4 \times 10^{-4}} = 4285 \text{ Pa} \approx \mathbf{4.3 \text{ kPa}}$$

Question 3: A

Assuming total energy is conserved, and it consists of only potential and kinetic energy, then at D the potential energy is highest compared to the other points as it is at the furthest distance from S. Hence, kinetic energy here is at its lowest (which means that it moves at its slowest).

PAT PAST PAPER SOLUTIONS 2006

Question 4: C

According to Archimedes' principle, the buoyancy force exerted on the object is equal to the weight of the fluid displaced by the object. This force must then be equal to the weight of the object as the object is in equilibrium (floating). Hence $mg = V_d \rho_w g$ where V_d is the displaced volume, m is the mass of the boat and ρ_w is the density of the water. Thus, $V_d = \frac{m}{\rho_w}$. The mass of the spoon of water is $\delta m = \rho_w \delta V$ and so $V'_d = \frac{m + \rho_w \delta V}{\rho_w} = V_d + \delta_V$. This means that more water is being displaced from the bath, increasing its water level. However, as the additional water was taken from the bath itself, then the displaced volume of the bath is $V_B = V_d + \delta V - \delta V = V_d$. So, **the water level stays the same.**

Question 5: B

In this question, the kinetic energy gained by the electron is derived from electrical energy due to the applied potential. Electrical energy is given by $E = eV$. Kinetic energy is given as

$$\frac{1}{2}mv^2 = \frac{(mv)^2}{2m} = \frac{p^2}{2m} = \frac{h^2}{2m\lambda^2}$$

Equating kinetic and electrical energy gives

$$\frac{h^2}{2m\lambda^2} = eV$$

$$\lambda^2 = \frac{h^2}{2meV}$$

$$\lambda = \frac{h}{\sqrt{2meV}}$$

Question 6: D

For steady acceleration, distance travelled can be expressed as

$$d = \frac{(u+v)t}{2}$$

u and v are the same in both cases, and with the second car t is double that of the first. The distance travelled by the second car is therefore double the distance travelled by the first car, so **2d**.

Question 7: C

Each distance is proportional to the square of its position in the sequence: $D \propto n^2$, whilst each year length is proportional to its position in the sequence cubed: $Y \propto n^3$. Therefore

$$n \propto \sqrt{D} \propto \sqrt[3]{Y}$$

$$Y \propto D^{\frac{3}{2}}$$

$$Y = kD\sqrt{D}$$

Question 8: C

The reading on the scale, R, will show the Martian's weight divided by the gravitational strength at the surface of Venus, as the scale was designed to be used on Venus. Hence,

$$R = \frac{m \times g_{Mars}}{g_{Venus}}$$

$$m = \frac{R \times g_{Venus}}{g_{Mars}} = \frac{93 \times 8.8}{3.8} = \mathbf{215\ kg}$$

PAT PAST PAPER SOLUTIONS   2006

Question 9: B

Mass will remain constant as there is no loss or gain of matter. Given that the mass remains constant, the smaller volume must mean that **the density has increased.**

Question 10: C

Taking downwards as positive, the initial velocity of the sandbag is 11 ms^{-1}. Use the equation $s = ut + \frac{1}{2}at^2$ to calculate the distance the sandbag has fallen in a time of 7 s:

$$s = 11 \times 7 + \frac{1}{2} \times 10 \times 7^2 = 77 + 245 = \textbf{322 m}$$

END OF SECTION

SECTION B

Question 11

The important thing to note here is that brightness depends on the power delivered to the lamp: $P = \dfrac{V^2}{R}$. Hence:

Lightbulb **a** will be dimmer than normal, as the potential from the cell is now divided across two identical bulbs.

Lightbulb **b** will be normal, as there is twice the voltage across two bulbs, so the voltage across each bulb will be the same.

Lightbulb **c** will be normal, as no current will flow through lightbulb **d**. This is because the potentials of the two cells act in opposite directions on **d**, and so there is no potential difference across it. This therefore means that lightbulb **d** is off.

Lightbulb **e** will be dimmer as the voltage from the cell is shared with the other lightbulb in series with **e**. Lightbulb **f** will be normal as it is in parallel with the cell, hence the voltage across the lightbulb is the same as the cell's potential.

Lightbulb **g** will be brighter as it has twice the potential difference across it. The voltage across **h** and the lightbulb in series with it is the potential difference from both cells combined, hence the voltage is shared and so **h** has normal brightness.

Question 12

In this question, there are five unknowns, which are the sides of red, green and blue cubes (r, g, and b respectively), their density (ρ_{cube}) and the density of the liquid (ρ_{liquid}). All cubes have the same density as all three of them float with half their volume exposed. This also shows that the liquid density must be twice the cube density:

$$\rho_{liquid} = 2\rho_{cube} \quad (1)$$

Putting the information in the question into the equations gives

(a) $r + g = 35$ (cm) (2)

(b) $2g + b = 70$ (cm) (3)

(c) $r + b = 2g$ (4)

(d) $\rho_{cube}(r^3 + g^3 + b^3) = 20{,}000$ (g) (5)

There are now five equations for the five unknowns, so they can be solved:

$$(3) - (4): 2g - r = 70 - 2g$$

$$4g - r = 70 \quad (6)$$

$$(2) + (6): 5g = 105$$

$$g = 21 \text{ cm}$$

Substituting back into (6) gives

$$r = 4 \times 21 - 70 = 14 \text{ cm}$$

Substituting into (4) then (5) gives

$$b = 2 \times 21 - 14 = 28 \text{ cm}$$

$$\rho_{cube}(14^3 + 21^3 + 28^3) = 20{,}000$$

$$\rho_{cube} = 0.589 \text{ g/cm}^3$$

Finally, in (1):

$$\rho_{liquid} = 2 \times 0.589 = \mathbf{1.178 \text{ g/cm}^3}$$

Question 13

a) At point X, the rocket must have reached its maximum velocity and started to slow down.

b) Acceleration is the derivative of velocity, and so the value of acceleration is given by the gradient of the velocity-time graph at any point. It is clear that this gradient is a maximum just before X, so this is when acceleration is also at a maximum. The maximum acceleration occurs at this point because all fuel has been used up, and so the total mass of the rocket is at its lowest value.

c) After point X, the gradient of the graph is constant and negative. This means that the rocket has constant deceleration.

d) Total displacement is obtained by integrating velocity with respect to time, so this can be calculated by estimating the area under the velocity-time graph. The rocket continues to rise while it still has positive velocity, so the second part of the curve (the straight line) should be extended until it reaches the x-axis.

END OF SECTION

PAT PAST PAPER SOLUTIONS — 2006

SECTION C

Question 14

a) Electrical energy is given by $E = Pt$ where t is time. As the question assumes 100% efficiency,

$$KE = Pt$$

$$\frac{1}{2}mv^2 = Pt$$

$$v = \sqrt{\frac{2Pt}{m}}$$

b) Acceleration is the derivate of velocity with respect to time:

$$a = \frac{dv}{dt} = \sqrt{\frac{2P}{m}}\left(\frac{1}{2}\right)t^{-\frac{1}{2}} = \sqrt{\frac{P}{2mt}}$$

Distance travelled is the integral of velocity with respect to time:

$$s = \int_0^t v\, dt = \sqrt{\frac{2P}{m}} \int_0^t t^{\frac{1}{2}}\, dt = \sqrt{\frac{2P}{m}}\left(\frac{2}{3}\right)t^{\frac{3}{2}} = \frac{2}{3}\sqrt{\frac{2Pt^3}{m}}$$

c) From the velocity expression in part (a), as $t \to \infty$, $v \to \infty$. This is **not reasonable**, as it is impossible to have infinite velocity.

d) From the acceleration expression in part (b), **as $t \to \infty$, $a \to 0$**. This is reasonable as an object cannot accelerate forever. **As $t \to 0$, $a \to \infty$** which is also reasonable, as it demonstrates rapid initial acceleration.

e) In this case, electrical energy is converted to gravitational potential energy:

$$Pt = mgh$$

$$h = \frac{Pt}{mg}$$

$$v_y = \frac{h}{t} = \frac{P}{mg}$$

f) Using the equation for vertical velocity derived in part (e),

$$KE_y = \frac{1}{2}mv_y^2 = \frac{1}{2}m\left(\frac{P}{mg}\right)^2 = \frac{P^2}{2mg^2}$$

The ratio of KE_y to GPE is therefore

$$\frac{KE_y}{GPE} = \frac{P^2/2mg^2}{Pt} = \frac{P}{2mg^2 t}$$

It is reasonable to ignore kinetic energy when this ratio is small, which occurs when P is small and t is large.

END OF SECTION

PAT PAST PAPER SOLUTIONS — 2006

MATHEMATICS FOR PHYSICS

Question 1

i) This is the difference of two squares:

$$2007^2 - 2006^2 = (2007 + 2006)(2007 - 2006)$$

$$= 4013 \times 1 = \mathbf{4013}$$

ii) Use the binomial expansion for both terms:

$$1.001^6 - 1.001^5 = (1 + 0.001)^6 - (1 + 0.001)^5$$

$$= (1 + 6 \times 0.001 + 15 \times 0.001^2 + \cdots)$$
$$- (1 + 5 \times 0.001 + 10 \times 0.001^2 + \cdots)$$

To one significant figure, only the first two terms of each expansion are required. Hence,

$$1.001^6 - 1.001^5 \approx (1 + 0.006) - (1 + 0.005) = \mathbf{0.001}$$

Question 2

The gradient of a straight line between two points is given by

$$m = \frac{y_2 - y_1}{x_2 - x_1} = \frac{-2 - 8}{5 - 4} = \frac{-10}{1} = \mathbf{-10}$$

Question 3

i) Use the log rule: $\log_a(a^n) = n$.

$$\log_e(e^{3x}) = 6$$

$$3x = 6$$

$$x = 2$$

ii) Use the definition of a log:

$$\log_3(x^2) = 2$$

$$x^2 = 3^2 = 9$$

$$x = \pm 3$$

Question 4

Consider the question in the context of the right-angled triangle below.

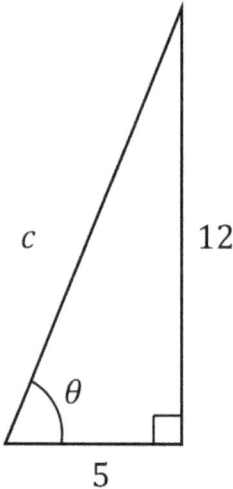

c can be found using Pythagoras' Theorem:

$$c^2 = 5^2 + 12^2 = 169$$

$$c = 13$$

In this case, $\theta = \tan^{-1}\left(\frac{12}{5}\right)$ and so

$$13\sin\left[\tan^{-1}\left(\frac{12}{5}\right)\right] = 13\sin\theta = 13\left(\frac{12}{13}\right) = 12$$

Question 5

i) This sketch is similar to the graph of $y = \sin x$, but is always positive and has steeper gradients:

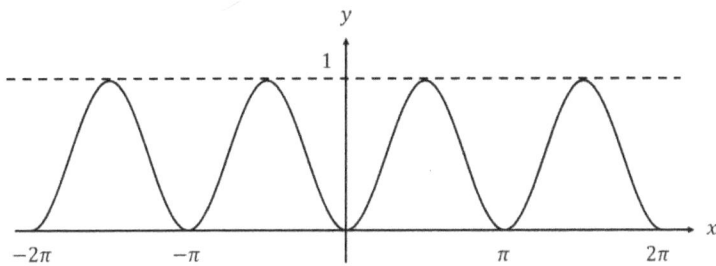

ii) Consider the points where the function intersects the x and y axes, and where it has asymptotes. When $x = 0$, $y = 1$ and when $y = 0$, x has no solutions. As $x \to \infty$ and $x \to -\infty$, $y \to 0$ (+ve) and so the x-axis is a horizontal asymptote. Vertical asymptotes exist where the denominator of the function is equal to zero. Therefore, at $x = \pm 1$, there are vertical asymptotes.

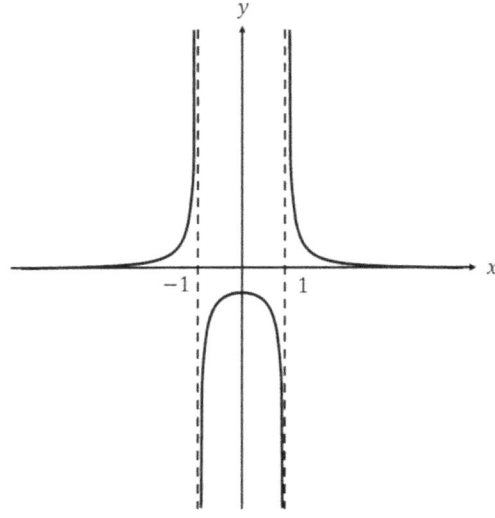

Question 6

The two statements can be written mathematically as follows:

(1) $r_A = r_B + 1$

(2) $\pi r_A^2 = \pi r_B^2 + 2\pi$

Substituting (1) into (2) gives

$$\pi(r_B + 1)^2 = \pi r_B^2 + 2\pi$$

$$r_B^2 + 2r_B + 1 = r_B^2 + 2$$

$$r_B = 0.5 \text{ cm}$$

Substituting back into (1) gives $r_A = 1.5$ cm.

Question 7

i) The probability of a 6 on any given roll is $\frac{1}{6}$. Since the rolls are independent, the individual probabilities of an event can be multiplied. Hence, the probability of three sixes is $\left(\frac{1}{6}\right)^3 = \frac{1}{216}$.

ii) As shown in part (i), the probability of all three dice giving a specific number is $\frac{1}{216}$. Since there are 6 different scenarios (due to 6 different possible numbers), the probability of the dice giving the same number three times is $6 \times \frac{1}{216} = \frac{1}{36}$.

iii) The probability of a roll not being a 6 is $\frac{5}{6}$. Therefore, the probability that only the third die gives a six is

$$\frac{5}{6} \times \frac{5}{6} \times \frac{1}{6} = \frac{25}{216}$$

PAT PAST PAPER SOLUTIONS 2006

Question 8

The question states that $\frac{dV}{dt} = 1 \text{ cm}^3\text{s}^{-1}$. To find rate of growth of radius, $\frac{dr}{dt}$, express V as a function of the radius: $V = \frac{4}{3}\pi r^3$. Differentiating this with respect to the radius gives $\frac{dV}{dr} = 4\pi r^2 = S = 100 \text{ cm}^2$, where S is the surface area of the balloon. Finally,

$$\frac{dr}{dt} = \frac{dr}{dV} \times \frac{dV}{dt} = \frac{1}{100} \times 1 = \mathbf{0.01 \text{ cms}^{-1}}$$

Question 9

The sketch of these lines is shown below.

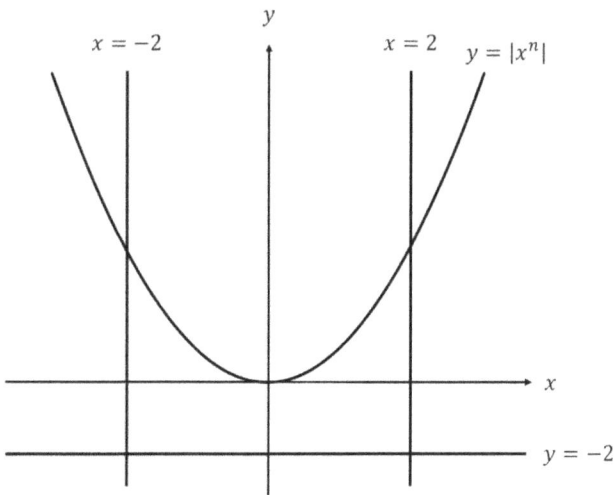

The area defined is equal to a rectangle under the x-axis plus the area between the curve $y = |x^n|$ and the x-axis.

The area is therefore given by

$$A = (4 \times 2) + \int_{-2}^{2} |x^n|\, dx = 8 + 2\int_{0}^{2} x^n\, dx$$

$$= 8 + 2\left[\frac{x^{n+1}}{n+1}\right]_0^2 = 8 + 2\left(\frac{2^{n+1}}{n+1}\right) = 8 + \frac{2^{n+2}}{n+1}$$

Question 10

i) $1 + e^y + e^{2y} + e^{3y} + \cdots$ is a geometric series with $r = e^y$. Since $r \ll 1$, then $S_\infty = \frac{a}{1-r} = \frac{1}{1-e^y}$

ii) Writing out the series by calculating each term gives

$$0 + 1 + 2 + \cdots + n$$

This is therefore an arithmetic series with common difference $d = 1$, first term $a = 0$ and number of terms $N = n + 1$.

$$S_N = \frac{N}{2}(a + (N-1)d)$$

$$S_N = \frac{n+1}{2} \times (0 + n) = \frac{n(n+1)}{2}$$

Question 11

To identify stationary points, differentiate the function and set it to zero:

$$\frac{dy}{dx} = 24 - 18x - 6x^2 = 0$$

$$x^2 + 3x - 4 = 0$$

$$(x+4)(x-1) = 0$$

$$x = -4, x = 1$$

To classify the nature of the stationary point, find the second differential at the turning point. If the second differential is positive, then it must be a minimum point, and if it is negative then it must be a maximum.

$$\frac{d^2y}{dx^2} = -18 - 12x$$

When $x = -4$, $y = -107$ and $\frac{d^2y}{dx^2} = 30$, hence $(-4, -107)$ **is a minimum point.**

When $x = 1$, $y = 18$ and $\frac{d^2y}{dx^2} = -30$, hence $(1, 18)$ **is a maximum point.**

Question 12

Let the square have side length x, and let the distance from the centre of the large and small circles to the nearest vertex be a and b respectively:

Consider the smaller circle:

$$b^2 = r^2 + r^2$$

$$b = \sqrt{2}r$$

Similarly for the larger circle,

$$a^2 = (2r)^2 + (2r)^2$$

$$a = 2\sqrt{2}r$$

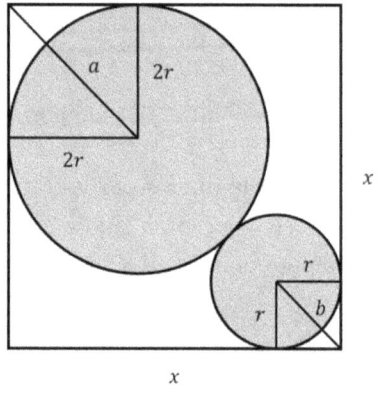

Since the diagonal of the square is equal to $a + 2r + r + b$,

$$x^2 + x^2 = (a + 2r + r + b)^2$$

$$2x^2 = r^2(2\sqrt{2} + 2 + 1 + \sqrt{2})^2$$

$$x^2 = \frac{r^2(3 + 3\sqrt{2})^2}{2}$$

The fraction of the area occupied by the circles is therefore

$$\frac{\pi(2r)^2 + \pi r^2}{x^2} = \frac{2 \times 5\pi r^2}{r^2(3 + 3\sqrt{2})^2} = \frac{10\pi}{27 + 18\sqrt{2}}$$

END OF PAPER

2007

PHYSICS

PART A

Question 1: C

Resistance is given by $R = \frac{\rho L}{A}$, where L is length and A is cross-sectional area. In this case,

$$R = \frac{\rho x}{x^2} = \frac{\rho}{x}$$

Therefore resistance is **inversely proportional to x**.

Question 2: D

The astronaut experiences weightlessness in the ISS because she is **accelerating at the same rate as the space station**. Gravitational acceleration provides the same centripetal acceleration to keep both the astronaut and the ISS in orbit around the Earth, and so this is what causes the feeling of weightlessness.

Question 3: A

The current flowing through the resistor is $I = \frac{V}{R} = \frac{9}{100} = 0.09$ A. Since $q = It$, the rate of flow of charge is 0.09 Cs^{-1}. Given that the charge of an electron is 1.6×10^{-19} C, the number of electrons passing through the resistor per second is

$$n = \frac{0.09}{1.6 \times 10^{-19}} = \mathbf{5.6 \times 10^{17}}$$

Question 4: C

As the slide curves into a gentler slope, a smaller component of the child's weight will be acting parallel to the slope, and so his **acceleration will decrease**. Since the child's acceleration is still positive, however, his **velocity will increase**.

Question 5: A

When two identical springs are connected in series, a force that would have produced an extension of x in one spring now causes an overall extension of $2x$. Hence,

$$kx = k'(2x)$$

$$k' = \frac{k}{2}$$

Question 6: A

Power dissipated is given by $P = \frac{V^2}{R}$. Since each resistor has a voltage V across it, the power dissipated in resistors R_1 and R_2 is $\frac{V^2}{R_1}$ and $\frac{V^2}{R_2}$ respectively. Hence, the total power dissipated is

$$P_{tot} = \frac{V^2}{R_1} + \frac{V^2}{R_2} = V^2 \left(\frac{1}{R_1} + \frac{1}{R_2} \right)$$

Question 7: B

As half of the drug is excreted by the body every two hours, and the isotope itself decays with a half-life of two hours, then overall the time taken for the quantity of radioactive drug to halve is

$$2 \times \frac{1}{2} = 1 \text{ hour}$$

Question 8: C

$$P = \frac{F}{A} = \frac{mg}{\pi r^2}$$

$$P = \frac{0.125 \times 10}{\pi (0.001)^2} = 397{,}887 \text{ Pa} \approx \mathbf{400 \text{ kPa}}$$

Question 9: A

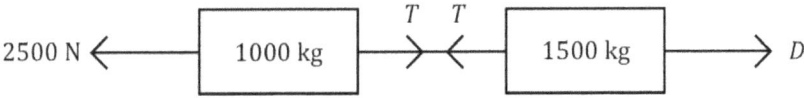

Consider only the trailer:

$$F = ma$$

$$T - 2500 = 1000 \times 4$$

$$T = 4000 + 2500 = \mathbf{6500 \text{ N}}$$

END OF SECTION

PART B

Question 10

a) The time taken is

$$t = \frac{d}{v} = \frac{300}{170} = 1.76 \text{ hours} \approx 106 \text{ mins}$$

The estimated time of arrival is therefore **10:46 am.**

b)

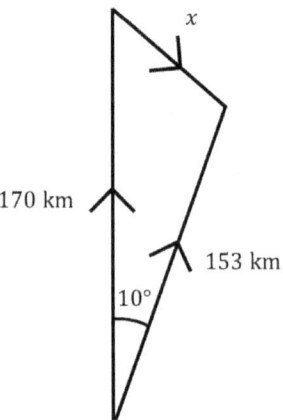

If there was no wind, the pilot would have travelled a distance of 170 km north in one hour. Using the cosine rule,

$$x^2 = 170^2 + 153^2 - 2 \times 170 \times 153 \times \cos 10$$

$$x = 32.9 \text{ km}$$

Since this is the distance offset by the wind in one hour, the wind speed must be **32.9 km/h.**

Question 11

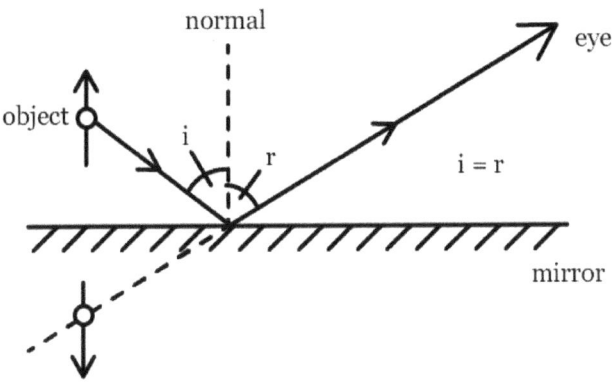

Question 12

Writing the information given in (a) – (c) mathematically gives

(a): $5m = 7v$ (1)

(b): $3l + m = 8v$ (2)

(c): $5l + 5m + 2v = 1$ (3)

where m, l and v are the lengths of mauve, lavender and violet caterpillars respectively. Substitute (1) into (2):

$$3l + \frac{7v}{5} = 8v$$

$$5l = 11v \quad (4)$$

Substitute (1) and (4) into (3):

$$11v + 7v + 2v = 1$$

$$v = 0.05 \text{ m}$$

Using (d),

$$v_l = \frac{0.05}{10} = 0.005 \text{ ms}^{-1}$$

Therefore $v_v = v_m = 0.01$ ms^{-1}. The time taken for a mauve caterpillar to crawl around the equator would therefore be

$$t = \frac{2\pi R}{v_m} = \frac{2\pi \times 1180 \times 10^3}{0.01} = 7.41 \times 10^8 \text{ s}$$

Question 13

When there is a current of 0.40 A flowing, the voltage across the non-linear resistor is given by

$$0.40 = 0.05 \times V_1^3$$

$$V_1 = \sqrt[3]{\frac{0.4}{0.05}} = 2 \text{ V}$$

The voltage across the fixed resistor must therefore be $V_2 = 9 - 2 = 7$ V. Using Ohm's law,

$$R_2 = \frac{V_2}{I}$$

$$R_2 = \frac{7}{0.4} = 17.5 \text{ }\Omega$$

END OF SECTION

PART C

Question 14

a) For an ideal pendulum, we can ignore the mass of the rod and treat the bob as a unit mass. Hence, $L_{CM} = L$ and $I = ML^2$. Using the formula for the period of a general pendulum,

$$P = 2\pi \sqrt{\frac{ML^2}{gML}} = 2\pi \sqrt{\frac{L}{g}}$$

b) For a pendulum made of a uniform rod, the centre of mass must be the middle of the rod, so $L_{CM} = \frac{L}{2}$. As given in the question, the inertia of the rod would be $I = \frac{1}{3}ML^2$.

$$P = 2\pi \sqrt{\frac{\frac{1}{3}ML^2}{gM\frac{1}{2}L}} = 2\pi \sqrt{\frac{2L}{3g}}$$

c) To find the effective length, consider the location of the centre of mass:

$$(M_b + M_r)L_{CM} = M_b L + M_r \frac{L}{2}$$

$$L_{CM} = L \left(\frac{M_b + \frac{M_r}{2}}{M_b + M_r} \right)$$

The total moment of inertia is found by summing the values for the component parts:

$$I = M_b L^2 + \frac{1}{3} M_r L^2 = L^2 \left(M_b + \frac{M_r}{3} \right)$$

~ 33 ~

The period of the pendulum can then be calculated using the general formula:

$$P = 2\pi \sqrt{\frac{L^2\left(M_b + \frac{M_r}{3}\right)}{g(M_b + M_r)L\left(\frac{M_b + \frac{M_r}{2}}{M_b + M_r}\right)}}$$

$$P = 2\pi \sqrt{\frac{L\left(M_b + \frac{M_r}{3}\right)}{g\left(M_b + \frac{M_r}{2}\right)}} = 2\pi \sqrt{\frac{2L(3M_b + M_r)}{3g(2M_b + M_r)}}$$

For an ideal pendulum, $M_r \to 0$:

$$P \to 2\pi \sqrt{\frac{2L(3M_b)}{3g(2M_b)}} = 2\pi \sqrt{\frac{L}{g}}$$

For a rod pendulum, $M_b \to 0$:

$$P \to 2\pi \sqrt{\frac{2L(M_r)}{3g(M_r)}} = 2\pi \sqrt{\frac{2L}{3g}}$$

d) Use the formula for the period of an ideal pendulum:

$$P = 2\pi \sqrt{\frac{L}{g}}$$

When there is an increase in temperature of δT,

~ 34 ~

$$P' = 2\pi \sqrt{\frac{L(1+\alpha\delta T)}{g}}$$

The error is therefore

$$\Delta P = P' - P = 2\pi \sqrt{\frac{L(1+\alpha\delta T)}{g}} - 2\pi \sqrt{\frac{L}{g}}$$

$$\Delta P = 2\pi \sqrt{\frac{L}{g}}(\sqrt{1+\alpha\delta T} - 1) = P(\sqrt{1+\alpha\delta T} - 1)$$

If the error after 24 hours is equal to one second,

$$\frac{\Delta P}{P} = \frac{1}{24 \times 60 \times 60} = \sqrt{1+\alpha\delta T} - 1$$

$$86400\sqrt{1+\alpha\delta T} = 1 + 86400$$

$$1 + \alpha\delta T = \left(\frac{86401}{86400}\right)^2$$

Given that $\alpha = 19 \times 10^{-6}$ K^{-1},

$$\delta T = \frac{1}{19 \times 10^{-6}}\left(\left(\frac{86401}{86400}\right)^2 - 1\right) = \mathbf{1.22\ K}$$

e) When $\alpha = 1.2 \times 10^{-6}$ K^{-1},

$$\delta T = \frac{1}{1.2 \times 10^{-6}}\left(\left(\frac{86401}{86400}\right)^2 - 1\right) = \mathbf{19.3\ K}$$

END OF SECTION

PAT PAST PAPER SOLUTIONS — 2007

MATHEMATICS FOR PHYSICS

Question 1

This is the difference of two squares:

$$6667^2 - 3333^2 = (6667 + 3333)(6667 - 3333)$$

$$= 10{,}000 \times 3{,}334 = \mathbf{33{,}340{,}000}$$

Question 2

First, find the gradient of the tangent by differentiating the equation of the curve:

$$\frac{dy}{dx} = 4x^3$$

$$m = \left.\frac{dy}{dx}\right|_{x=-2} = 4(-2)^3 = -32$$

The equation of the tangent is therefore

$$(y - y_1) = m(x - x_1)$$

$$(y - 16) = -32(x - (-2))$$

$$\mathbf{y = -32x - 48}$$

Question 3

Write 125 and 25 as powers of 5, and then use log rules to simplify:

$$\frac{2 \log 125}{3 \log 25} = \frac{2 \log(5^3)}{3 \log(5^2)} = \frac{3 \times 2 \log 5}{2 \times 3 \log 5} = \frac{6}{6} = \mathbf{1}$$

Question 4

i) There are five possible combinations where the dice add up to 6: $(1 + 5)$, $(2 + 4)$, $(3 + 3)$, $(4 + 2)$ and $(5 + 1)$. Each of these combinations has a probability of $\frac{1}{6} \times \frac{1}{6} = \frac{1}{36}$ occurring, so the overall probability is $5 \times \frac{1}{36} = \frac{5}{36}$.

ii) Similarly, there are two combinations that add up to 11: $(5 + 6)$ and $(6 + 5)$. The probability is therefore $2 \times \frac{1}{36} = \frac{1}{18}$.

Question 5

This is a binomial expansion:

$$(2 + x)^5 = 2^5 + (5)(2)^4 x + (10)(2)^3 (x)^2 + (10)(2)^2 (x)^3 + \cdots$$
$$= \mathbf{32 + 80x + 80x^2 + 40x^3 + \cdots}$$

Question 6

i) From the sketch here, we can see that $\sin 30 = \frac{r_s}{r_l} = \frac{1}{2}$ and therefore $r_l = 2r_s$. The ratio of the circles is therefore

$$\frac{A_l}{A_s} = \frac{\pi r_l^2}{\pi r_s^2} = 2^2 = 4$$

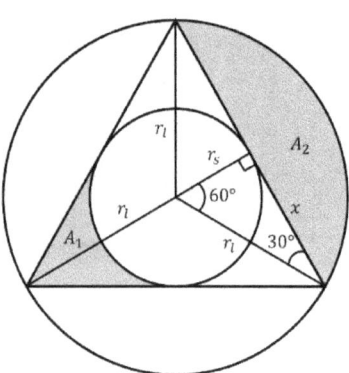

ii) The height of the triangle is given by $r_s + r_l$. We can also see that $\tan 30 = \frac{r_s}{x}$, so $x = r_s\sqrt{3}$. Hence the area of the triangle is

$$A_t = \frac{1}{2} \times 2x \times (r_s + r_l) = \sqrt{3}r_s(r_s + r_l)$$

We can then see that $A_1 = \frac{A_t - A_s}{3}$ and that $A_2 = \frac{A_l - A_t}{3}$. The ratio of the two areas is therefore

$$\frac{A_2}{A_1} = \frac{A_l - A_t}{A_t - A_s} = \frac{\pi r_l^2 - \sqrt{3}r_s(r_s + r_l)}{\sqrt{3}r_s(r_s + r_l) - \pi r_s^2}$$

$$= \frac{\pi r_l^2 - \sqrt{3}r_s^2 - \sqrt{3}r_s r_l}{\sqrt{3}r_s^2 + \sqrt{3}r_s r_l - \pi r_s^2}$$

$$= \frac{\pi(2r_s)^2 - \sqrt{3}r_s^2 - \sqrt{3}r_s(2r_s)}{\sqrt{3}r_s^2 + \sqrt{3}r_s(2r_s) - \pi r_s^2}$$

$$= \frac{r_s^2\left(4\pi - \sqrt{3} - 2\sqrt{3}\right)}{r_s^2\left(\sqrt{3} + 2\sqrt{3} - \pi\right)} = \frac{4\pi - 3\sqrt{3}}{3\sqrt{3} - \pi}$$

Question 7

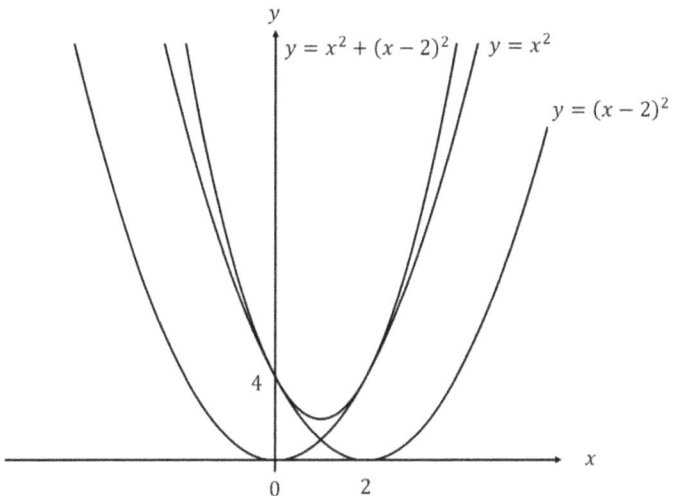

$y = (x - 2)^2$ is the same as the $y = x^2$ curve but shifted by 2 along the x-axis. $y = x^2 + (x - 2)^2$ is the sum of these two curves, which gives the curve in the middle.

Question 8

$$\tan\theta = 2\sin\theta$$

$$\frac{\sin\theta}{\cos\theta} = 2\sin\theta$$

$$\sin\theta(2\cos\theta - 1) = 0$$

$$\sin\theta = 0 \text{ or } \cos\theta = \frac{1}{2}$$

When $\sin\theta = 0$, $\theta = 0, \pi, 2\pi$ and when $\cos\theta = \frac{1}{2}$, $\theta = \frac{\pi}{3}, \frac{5\pi}{3}$. Therefore,

$$\theta = 0, \frac{\pi}{3}, \pi, \frac{5\pi}{3}, 2\pi$$

Question 9

Let **a** be the vector connecting the points $(-1,-2)$ and $(-5,4)$ and **b** be the vector connecting the points $(-1,-2)$ and $(5,2)$:

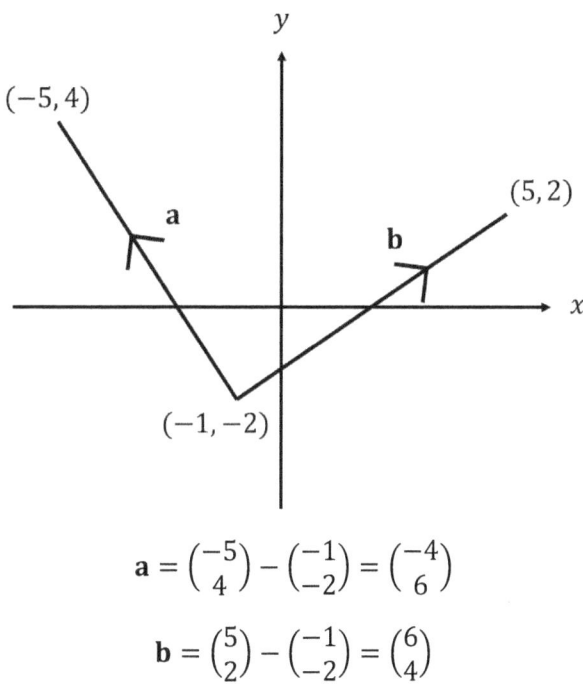

$$\mathbf{a} = \begin{pmatrix} -5 \\ 4 \end{pmatrix} - \begin{pmatrix} -1 \\ -2 \end{pmatrix} = \begin{pmatrix} -4 \\ 6 \end{pmatrix}$$

$$\mathbf{b} = \begin{pmatrix} 5 \\ 2 \end{pmatrix} - \begin{pmatrix} -1 \\ -2 \end{pmatrix} = \begin{pmatrix} 6 \\ 4 \end{pmatrix}$$

To show that these three points lie at three corners of a square, two conditions must be proven:

1) **a** and **b** must have equal magnitude, and

2) **a** and **b** must be perpendicular.

$$|\mathbf{a}| = \sqrt{(-4)^2 + 6^2} = \sqrt{52}$$

$$|\mathbf{b}| = \sqrt{6^2 + 4^2} = \sqrt{52}$$

∴ **a** and **b** have the same magnitude.

To find the angle between **a** and **b**, consider their dot product:

$$\mathbf{a} \cdot \mathbf{b} = \begin{pmatrix} -4 \\ 6 \end{pmatrix} \cdot \begin{pmatrix} 6 \\ 4 \end{pmatrix} = -24 + 24 = 0$$

Hence **a** and **b** are perpendicular and have equal length, so the three points must be the three corners of a square.

To find the fourth corner, add vector **b** to the point $(-5, 4)$:

$$\begin{pmatrix} -5 \\ 4 \end{pmatrix} + \mathbf{b} = \begin{pmatrix} -5 \\ 4 \end{pmatrix} + \begin{pmatrix} 6 \\ 4 \end{pmatrix} = \begin{pmatrix} 1 \\ 8 \end{pmatrix}$$

Finally, the area of the square is

$$|\mathbf{a}| \times |\mathbf{b}| = \left(\sqrt{52}\right)^2 = 52$$

Question 10

$$\int_1^9 \left(\sqrt{x} + \frac{1}{\sqrt{x}}\right) dx = \int_1^9 \left(x^{\frac{1}{2}} + x^{-\frac{1}{2}}\right) dx$$

$$= \left[\frac{2}{3} x^{\frac{3}{2}} + 2 x^{\frac{1}{2}}\right]_1^9 = \left(\frac{2}{3} \times 9^{\frac{3}{2}} + 2 \times 9^{\frac{1}{2}}\right) - \left(\frac{2}{3} \times 1 + 2 \times 1\right)$$

$$= \frac{2}{3} \times \left(\sqrt{9}\right)^3 + 2 \times \sqrt{9} - \frac{2}{3} - 2 = 18 + 6 - \frac{2}{3} - 2 = \frac{64}{3}$$

Question 11

From the statements in the question we can deduce:

$$ar = a + d$$

$$d = a(r - 1) \quad (1)$$

$$ar^2 = 2(a + 2d)$$

$$d = \frac{a(r^2 - 2)}{4} \quad (2)$$

Set (1) equal to (2):

$$a(r - 1) = \frac{a(r^2 - 2)}{4}$$

$$r - 1 = \frac{r^2 - 2}{4}$$

$$r^2 - 4r + 2 = 0$$

Solving this expression using the quadratic formula $\left(x = \frac{-b \pm \sqrt{b^2 - 4ac}}{2a}\right)$ gives

$$r = \frac{4 \pm \sqrt{16 - 8}}{2} = 2 \pm \sqrt{2}$$

Question 12

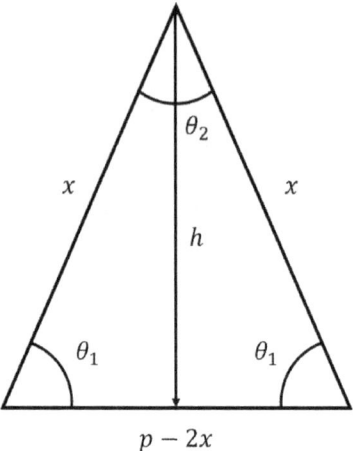

First, find the height of the triangle, h, in terms of x and p:

$$x^2 = h^2 + \left(\frac{p-2x}{2}\right)^2$$

$$h = \left[x^2 - \frac{1}{4}(p^2 - 4px + 4x^2)\right]^{\frac{1}{2}} = \left[x^2 - \frac{p^2}{4} + px - x^2\right]^{\frac{1}{2}}$$

$$h = \frac{1}{2}[4px - p^2]^{\frac{1}{2}}$$

Now, an expression for the area of the triangle can be obtained:

$$A = \frac{1}{2} \times (p - 2x) \times h$$

$$A = \frac{1}{4}(p - 2x)(4px - p^2)^{\frac{1}{2}}$$

Since p is fixed, maximum area is obtained by differentiating the expression with respect to x and setting it to zero.

PAT PAST PAPER SOLUTIONS — 2007

$$\frac{dA}{dx} = \frac{1}{4}\left[(p-2x)\left(\frac{1}{2}\right)(4p)(4px-p^2)^{-\frac{1}{2}} + (-2)(4px-p^2)^{\frac{1}{2}}\right] = 0$$

$$\frac{1}{4}(4px-p^2)^{-\frac{1}{2}}[2p(p-2x) - 2(4px-p^2)] = 0$$

$$\frac{1}{4}(4px-p^2)^{-\frac{1}{2}}[2p^2 - 4px - 8px + 2p^2] = 0$$

$$\frac{1}{4}\left(\frac{4p^2 - 12px}{\sqrt{4px-p^2}}\right) = \frac{p^2 - 3px}{\sqrt{4px-p^2}} = 0$$

$$p^2 - 3px = 0$$

$$x = \frac{p^2}{3p} = \frac{p}{3}$$

Since $p - 2x = \frac{p}{3} = x$, this in an equilateral triangle. This therefore means that

$$\theta_1 = \theta_2 = 60°$$

END OF PAPER

2008

PART A

Question 1

$1 + 2 + 3 + \cdots + 99 + 100$ is an arithmetic series with first term 1 and common difference 1. So,

$$S_n = \frac{n}{2}(a_1 + a_n)$$

$$S_{100} = \frac{100}{2}(1 + 100) = 50(101) = \mathbf{5050}$$

Question 2

$$(0.25)^{-\frac{1}{2}} = \left(\frac{1}{4}\right)^{-\frac{1}{2}} = 4^{\frac{1}{2}} = \sqrt{4} = 2$$

$$(0.09)^{\frac{3}{2}} = \left(\frac{9}{100}\right)^{\frac{3}{2}} = \left(\sqrt{\frac{9}{100}}\right)^3 = \left(\frac{3}{10}\right)^3 = \frac{27}{1000} = 0.027$$

Question 3

$$(1+a)^n \approx 1 + na + \frac{n(n-1)a^2}{2} + \cdots$$

For $(1+x)^{m+1}$, $a = x$ and $n = m+1$

For $(1-2x)^m$, $a = -2x$ and $n = m$

So,

$(1+x)^{m+1}(1-2x)^m$

$$\approx \left[1 + (m+1)x + \frac{(m+1)mx^2}{2}\right]\left[1 + m(-2x) + \frac{m(m-1)(-2x)^2}{2}\right]$$

$$= 1 + x(m+1-2m)$$
$$+ x^2\left(\frac{m(m+1)}{2} - 2m(m+1) + \frac{m(m-1)(-2)^2}{2}\right)$$

$$= 1 + (1-m)x + x^2\left(\frac{m^2}{2} + \frac{m}{2} - 2m^2 - 2m + 2m^2 - 2m\right)$$

$$= 1 + (1-m)x + \left(\frac{m^2 - 7m}{2}\right)x^2$$

Question 4

Both sides of the inequality can be multiplied by $(1 - x^2)^2$ as it is always positive:

$$\frac{x^2 + 2}{1 - x^2} < 3$$

$$(x^2 + 2)(1 - x^2) < 3(1 - x^2)^2$$

$$-x^4 - x^2 + 2 < 3 - 6x^2 + 3x^4$$

$$4x^4 - 5x^2 + 1 > 0$$

$$(4x^2 - 1)(x^2 - 1) > 0$$

$$(2x + 1)(2x - 1)(x + 1)(x - 1) > 0$$

For this expression to satisfy the inequality, either all four brackets are positive, two brackets are positive and two are negative, or all four brackets are negative. These solutions can be viewed on a number line:

	-1	$-\frac{1}{2}$	$\frac{1}{2}$	1	
$(x+1)$	$-$	$+$	$+$	$+$	$+$
$(2x+1)$	$-$	$-$	$+$	$+$	$+$
$(2x-1)$	$-$	$-$	$-$	$+$	$+$
$(x-1)$	$-$	$-$	$-$	$-$	$+$

Hence

$$x < -1, -\frac{1}{2} < x < \frac{1}{2}, x > 1$$

Question 5

For both parts, use the log rule

$$\log_a b = \frac{\log_c b}{\log_c a}$$

i) $\log_2 9 = \dfrac{\log_9 9}{\log_9 2} = \dfrac{1}{x}$

ii) $\log_8 3 = \dfrac{\log_9 3}{\log_9 8} = \dfrac{\log_9 \left(9^{\frac{1}{2}}\right)}{\log_9(2^3)} = \dfrac{1/2}{3\log_9 2} = \dfrac{1}{6x}$

Question 6

For $1, x^2, x$ to be successive terms of an arithmetic progression,

$$x^2 = 1 + d$$
$$d = x^2 - 1 \quad (1)$$
$$x = x^2 + d$$
$$d = x - x^2 \quad (2)$$

Equate (1) and (2):

$$x^2 - 1 = x - x^2$$
$$2x^2 - x - 1 = 0$$
$$(2x + 1)(x - 1) = 0$$
$$x = 1 \text{ or } x = -\frac{1}{2}$$

Question 7

The gradient of the curve at any point is given by

$$\frac{dy}{dx} = 1 + x + x^2 + x^3 + \cdots$$

The gradient of the straight line $y = ax$ is always a.

At $x = 0$, $\frac{dy}{dx} = 1$ and so $a = 1$.

At $x = \frac{1}{4}$, $\frac{dy}{dx}$ is a geometric series with $r = \frac{1}{4}$ and $a = 1$. Therefore

$$\frac{dy}{dx} = S_\infty = \frac{a}{1-r} = \frac{1}{1-\frac{1}{4}} = \frac{4}{3}$$

Hence, $a = \frac{4}{3}$.

Question 8

The centre of the circle must be the mid-point of the given coordinates:

$$(a, b) = \left(\frac{5-3}{2}, \frac{2+8}{2}\right) = (1, 5)$$

The diameter of the circle is the distance between the two points, and the radius is half this value:

$$r = \frac{1}{2}\sqrt{(5-(-3))^2 + (2-8)^2} = \frac{1}{2}\sqrt{100} = 5$$

Hence the equation of the circle is

$$(x-a)^2 + (y-b)^2 = r^2$$

$$(x-1)^2 + (y-5)^2 = 25$$

PAT PAST PAPER SOLUTIONS   2008

Question 9

Let the probability of rolling a 2 be $P(2) = a$. Then $P(3) = P(4) = a$, $P(5) = P(6) = 3a$ and $P(1) = 0$. All the probabilities must sum to 1:

$$a + a + a + 3a + 3a = 1$$

$$9a = 1 \rightarrow a = \frac{1}{9}$$

Hence, $P(1) = 0$, $P(2) = P(3) = P(4) = \frac{1}{9}$, $P(5) = P(6) = \frac{1}{3}$

i) $P(2) = \frac{1}{9}$

ii) To get a total of at least 10, only 4, 5 or 6 may be thrown. If a four is thrown, then the second roll must be a 6, if a five is thrown then the second roll must be a 5 or 6 and if a 6 is thrown then the second roll can be 4, 5 or 6.

$$P(\text{Sum} \geq 10) = [P(4) \times P(6)] + [P(5) \times (P(5) + P(6))]$$
$$+ [P(6) \times (P(4) + P(5) + P(6))]$$

$$= \left[\frac{1}{9} \times \frac{1}{3}\right] + \left[\frac{1}{3} \times \left(\frac{1}{3} + \frac{1}{3}\right)\right] + \left[\frac{1}{3} \times \left(\frac{1}{9} + \frac{1}{3} + \frac{1}{3}\right)\right]$$

$$= \frac{1}{27} + \frac{2}{9} + \frac{7}{27} = \frac{14}{27}$$

Question 10

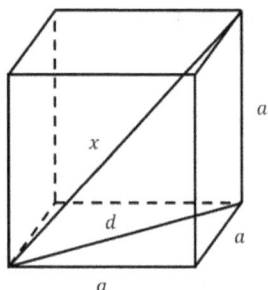

On the bottom face,

$$d^2 = a^2 + a^2 = 2a^2$$

Consider the right-angled triangle made by x, d and the vertical side a:

$$x^2 = a^2 + d^2 = 3a^2$$

$$x = \sqrt{3}a$$

Question 11

i) $\displaystyle\int_{-1}^{1} (x + x^3 + x^5 + x^7)\, dx = \left[\frac{x^2}{2} + \frac{x^4}{4} + \frac{x^6}{6} + \frac{x^8}{8}\right]_{-1}^{1}$

$$= \left(\frac{1}{2} + \frac{1}{4} + \frac{1}{6} + \frac{1}{8}\right) - \left(\frac{1}{2} + \frac{1}{4} + \frac{1}{6} + \frac{1}{8}\right) = 0$$

ii) $\displaystyle\int_{0}^{1} \left(\frac{x^9 + x^{99}}{11}\right) dx = \frac{1}{11}\left[\frac{x^{10}}{10} + \frac{x^{100}}{100}\right]_{0}^{1}$

$$= \frac{1}{11}\left(\frac{1}{10} + \frac{1}{100}\right) = \frac{1}{11}\left(\frac{11}{100}\right) = \frac{1}{100}$$

Question 12

First, consider the smaller triangle ABC:

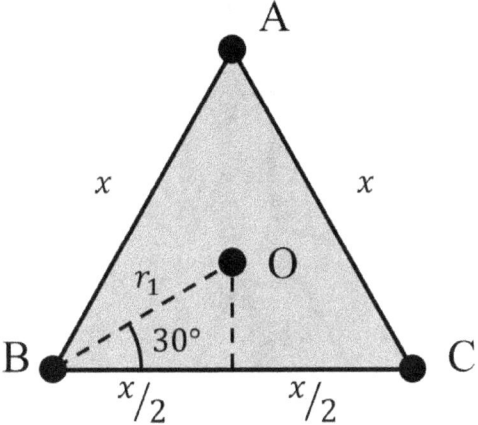

The area of the triangle is given by

$$A_{ABC} = \frac{1}{2}x^2 \sin 60 = \frac{\sqrt{3}}{4}x^2$$

The distance from the centre of the triangle to a vertex, r_1, is given by

$$\cos 30 = \frac{x/2}{r_1}$$

$$r_1 = \frac{x}{\sqrt{3}}$$

Hence, the area of the smaller circle is

$$A_1 = \pi r_1^2 = \frac{\pi x^2}{3}$$

Now consider the full shape:

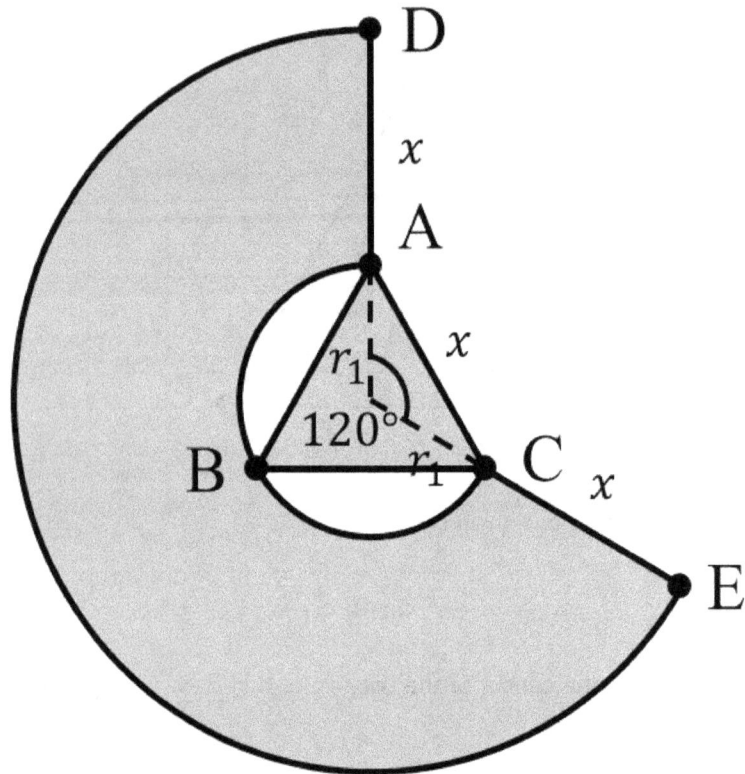

The radius of the larger circle is $r_2 = x + r_1 = x\left(1 + \frac{1}{\sqrt{3}}\right)$. Hence, the area of the larger circle is

$$A_2 = \pi r_2^2 = \pi x^2 \left(1 + \frac{1}{\sqrt{3}}\right)^2$$

$$A_2 = \pi x^2 \left(1 + \frac{2}{\sqrt{3}} + \frac{1}{3}\right) = 2\pi x^2 \left(\frac{2 + \sqrt{3}}{3}\right)$$

As angle AOC is 120°,

$$A_{\text{ADEC}} = \frac{240}{360}A_2 - A_1 = \frac{2}{3}\left[2\pi x^2 \left(\frac{2+\sqrt{3}}{3}\right) - \frac{\pi x^2}{3}\right]$$

$$A_{\text{ADEC}} = \frac{2\pi x^2}{9}(4 + 2\sqrt{3} - 1) = \frac{2\pi x^2}{9}(3 + 2\sqrt{3})$$

$$\frac{A_{\text{ADEC}}}{A_{\text{ABC}}} = \frac{2\pi x^2}{9}(3 + 2\sqrt{3}) \div \frac{\sqrt{3}}{4}x^2$$

$$\frac{A_{\text{ADEC}}}{A_{\text{ABC}}} = \frac{8\pi}{9\sqrt{3}}(3 + 2\sqrt{3}) = \frac{8\pi(\sqrt{3} + 2)}{9}$$

END OF SECTION

PART B

Question 13: D

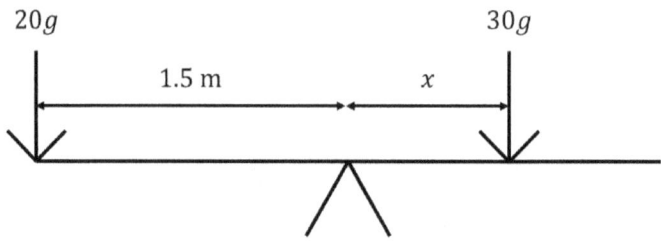

If the seesaw is balanced, clockwise and anticlockwise moments must be equal:

$$20g \times 1.5 = 30g \times x$$

$$x = 1 \text{ m}$$

Hence she must sit $x + 1.5 = \textbf{2.5 m}$ away from him.

Question 14: B

The released energy comes as a result of the decrease in mass.

Question 15: D

The total mass of stars in the universe is

$$M = 2 \times 10^{30} \times 250 \times 10^9 \times 400 \times 10^9 = 2 \times 10^{53} \text{ kg}$$

Mass of dark matter $= 20 \times M = 4 \times 10^{54}$ kg

Total mass of the universe $= \mathbf{4.2 \times 10^{54}}$ **kg**

Question 16: A

A solar eclipse occurs when the moon is between earth and the sun, hence the phase is **new moon**.

PAT PAST PAPER SOLUTIONS   2008

Question 17: C

There is no change in mass and the volume is fixed, so

$$\rho = \frac{m}{V} = \text{constant}$$

For an ideal gas, $pV = nRT$. Since V and n are fixed and R is constant,

$$\frac{p}{T} = \frac{nR}{V} = \text{constant}$$

$$p \propto T$$

Hence, as the temperature increases, pressure increases.

Question 18: B

The minimum energy required is the potential energy needed to climb the height:

$$GPE = mgh = 60 \times 10 \times 4 = \mathbf{2400\,J}$$

Question 19: C

Energy in the battery $= VIt = 3.6 \times 0.7 \times 3600 = 9072\,J$

Power output from the solar panel $= (0.25)^2 \times 1000 \times 0.1 = 6.25\,W$

Time taken to charge $= \frac{E}{P} = \frac{9072}{6.25} = 1451\,s = \mathbf{0.40\ hours}$.

Question 20: C

Power dissipated is given by $P = \frac{V^2}{R}$. Power is therefore maximised when resistance is lowest, which for a light dependent resistor is when incident light is at a maximum. This happens at **noon**.

Question 21: A

All kinetic energy must be converted to thermal energy of the water:

$$\frac{1}{2}m_b v^2 = m_w c \Delta T$$

$$\frac{1}{2} \times 0.01 \times 400^2 = 2^3 \times 1000 \times 4.2 \times 10^3 \times \Delta T$$

$$800 = 8 \times 4.2 \times 10^6 \times \Delta T$$

$$\Delta T = \frac{800}{8 \times 4.2 \times 10^6} = \frac{1}{4.2 \times 10^4} = \mathbf{2.4 \times 10^{-5}\ K}$$

Question 22: A

Since one gram is equal to 10^{-3} kg, both sides of the equation must be multiplied by 10^{-3} and so the units for energy in this case would be 10^{-3} J = **mJ**.

Question 23

Given that $q = CV$ and $C = \frac{\rho A}{d}$,

$$W = \frac{q^2}{2C} = \frac{(CV)^2}{2C} = \frac{CV^2}{2} = \frac{\rho A V^2}{2d}$$

Given that $V_{max} = Bd$,

$$E_{max} = \frac{\rho A V_{max}^2}{2d} = \frac{\rho A B^2 d^2}{2d} = \frac{\rho A B^2 d}{2}$$

Since the volume of the dielectric is Ad, this can be expressed in terms of the dielectric's mass and density:

$$D = \frac{m}{Ad} \rightarrow Ad = \frac{m}{D}$$

$$E_{max} = \frac{m\rho B^2}{2D}$$

For the values given in the question,

$$E_{max} = \frac{1 \times 2 \times 10^{-11} \times (2 \times 10^7)^2}{2 \times 1000} = 4\,\text{J}$$

Since $1\,\text{kW} = 1000\,\text{J/s}$, the 4 J capacity of the capacitor is too small to be useful.

Question 24

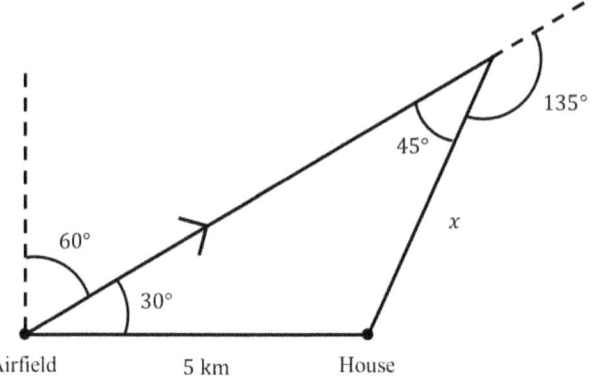

Use the sine rule:

$$\frac{x}{\sin 30} = \frac{5}{\sin 45}$$

$$x = \frac{5 \sin 30}{\sin 45} = \frac{5 \times \frac{1}{2}}{\frac{\sqrt{2}}{2}} = \frac{5}{\sqrt{2}} = \frac{5\sqrt{2}}{2}$$

$$x \approx 2.5 \times 1.4 = \mathbf{3.5 \text{ km}}$$

Question 25

Each statement can be formulated mathematically:

(a): $c + r = 2s$

$$r = 2s - c \qquad (1)$$

(b): $c^2 + s^2 = r^2 \qquad (2)$

(c): $2c + s = 1$

$$s = 1 - 2c \qquad (3)$$

Substitute (3) into (1):

$$r = 2(1 - 2c) - c$$
$$r = 2 - 5c \quad (4)$$

Substitute (3) and (4) into (2):

$$c^2 + (1 - 2c)^2 = (2 - 5c)^2$$
$$c^2 + 1 - 4c + 4c^2 = 4 - 20c + 25c^2$$
$$20c^2 - 16c + 3 = 0$$
$$(10c - 3)(2c - 1) = 0$$
$$c = \frac{3}{10} \text{ or } \frac{1}{2}$$

From (3), c cannot be $\frac{1}{2}$ as this would give $s = 0$. Substitute $c = 0.3$ m into (3) and (4):

$$c = 0.3 \text{ m}, s = 0.4 \text{ m}, r = 0.5 \text{ m}$$

Question 26

The most rapid change in height occurs where the gradient is the steepest, which is at approximately **7 am** in the morning.

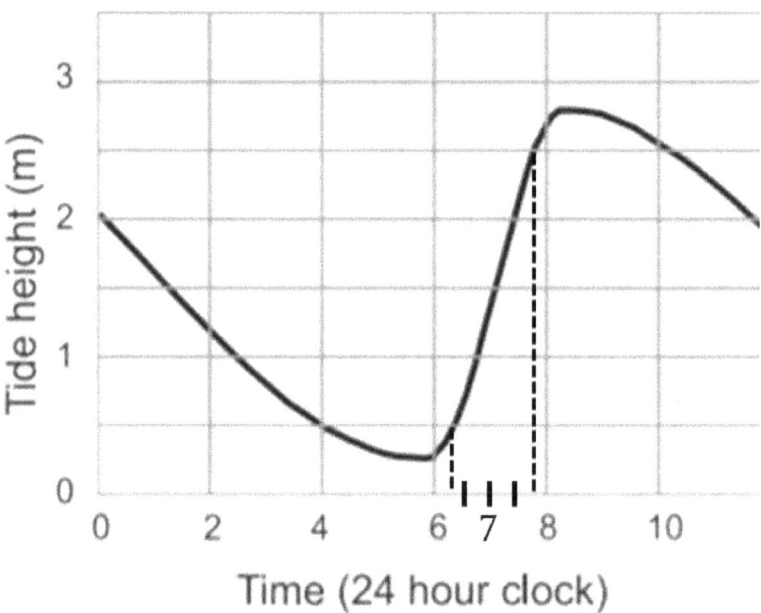

The gradient at this point can be estimated by considering the change in height and change in time over this point:

$$m = \frac{\Delta h}{\Delta t} = \frac{250 - 50}{7 \text{ hrs } 45 \text{ mins} - 6 \text{ hrs } 15 \text{ mins}} = \frac{200}{90}$$

$$= \frac{20}{9} \approx \mathbf{2.2 \text{ cm/min}}$$

PAT PAST PAPER SOLUTIONS 2008

Question 27

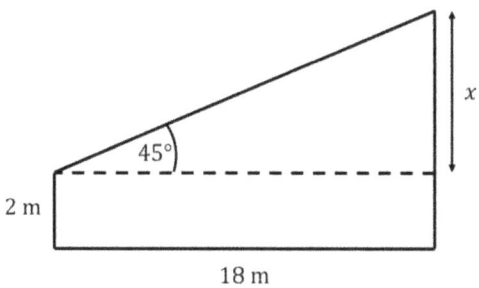

$$\tan 45 = \frac{x}{18} = 1$$

$$x = 18 \text{ m}$$

a) The height of the nest is $18 + 2 = 20$ m. Taking downwards as positive,

$$s = ut + \frac{1}{2}at^2$$

$$20 = \frac{1}{2} \times 10 \times t^2$$

$$t = \sqrt{4} = \mathbf{2 \text{ s}}$$

b)

$$v = u + at$$

$$v = 10 \times 2 = \mathbf{20 \text{ ms}^{-1}}$$

c) Since the work done on the egg is given by $W = Fd$,

$$KE = W$$

$$\frac{1}{2}mv^2 = Fd$$

$$\frac{1}{2} \times 0.02 \times 20^2 = F \times 10^{-3}$$

$$F = \frac{10^{-2} \times 400}{10^{-3}} = 4 \text{ kN}$$

d) Since $W = Fd$,

$$W = 4 \times 10^3 \times 10^{-3} = 4 \text{ J}$$

The initial GPE of the egg is

$$GPE = mgh = 0.02 \times 10 \times 20 = 4 \text{ J} = W$$

e) Now the egg is brought to a stop in a distance of 5 cm:

$$F = \frac{10^{-2} \times 400}{5 \times 10^{-2}} = 80 \text{ N}$$

The time taken can be found by considering the change in momentum of the egg (taking downwards as positive):

$$Ft = m(v - u)$$

$$-80 \times t = 0.02(0 - 20)$$

$$t = \frac{20 \times 2 \times 10^{-2}}{80} = 0.5 \times 10^{-2} = 5 \text{ ms}$$

f) The minimum energy required would be the gravitational potential energy:

$$E_{min} = mgh = (100 + 0.02) \times 10 \times 20$$

$$E_{min} \approx 100 \times 10 \times 20 = \mathbf{2 \times 10^4 \ J}$$

g) The energy required to heat the egg is given by $mc\Delta T$. Using the same E_{min},

$$E_{min} \times \text{efficiency} = mc\Delta T$$

$$\text{efficiency} = \frac{0.02 \times 4 \times 10^3 \times (100 - 20)}{2 \times 10^4}$$

$$= \frac{2 \times 10^{-2} \times 4 \times 10^3 \times 80}{2 \times 10^4} = 32 \times 10^{-2} = 0.32 = \mathbf{32\%}$$

END OF PAPER

PAT PAST PAPER SOLUTIONS 2009

2009
PART A

Question 1

$$y = \tan t = \frac{\sin t}{\cos t} = \frac{\sin t}{\sqrt{1 - \sin^2 t}} = \frac{x}{\sqrt{1 - x^2}}$$

Question 2

The graph of $y = x + \frac{4}{x^2}$ can be constructed by adding the two separate functions $y = x$ and $y = \frac{4}{x^2}$, both of which are shown below:

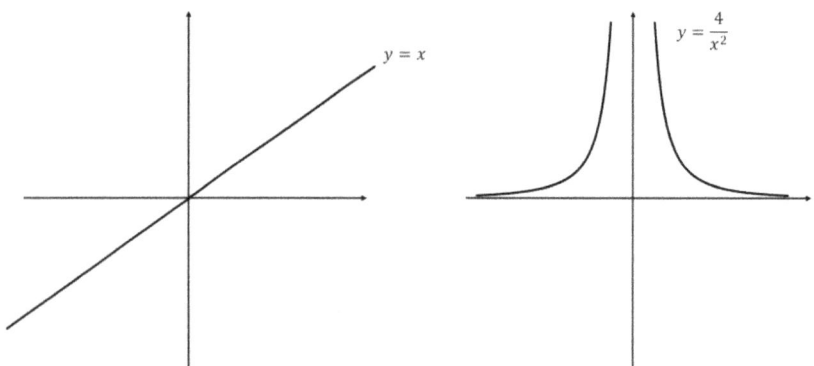

To find the stationary point of the combined function, differentiate the function and set it to zero:

$$y = x + 4x^{-2}$$

$$\frac{dy}{dx} = 1 - 8x^{-3} = 0$$

$$1 - \frac{8}{x^3} = 0$$

~ 66 ~

$$x^3 = 8$$

$$x = 2$$

At this point, $y = 2 + \frac{4}{2^2} = 3$. There is therefore a stationary point at $(2, 3)$. Finally, find the y value at the points $x = \pm 4$:

When $x = 4$, $y = 4 + \frac{4}{4^2} = 4.25$

When $x = -4$, $y = -4 + \frac{4}{(-4)^2} = -3.75$

The full sketch is then obtained by combining the two above graphs and incorporating these three points:

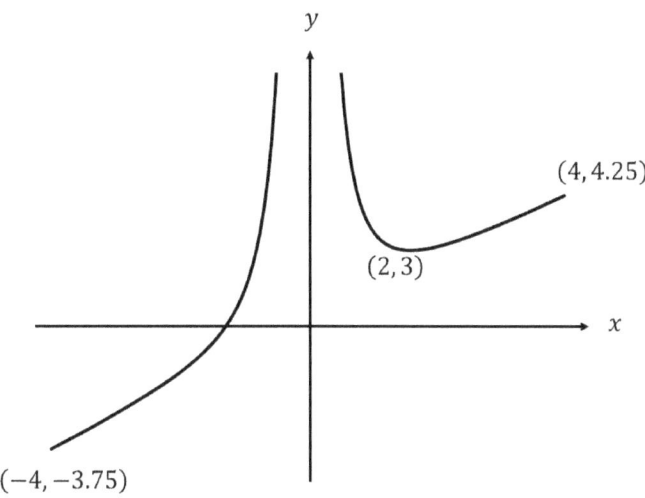

Question 3

A sketch of the circle and the two lines is shown below:

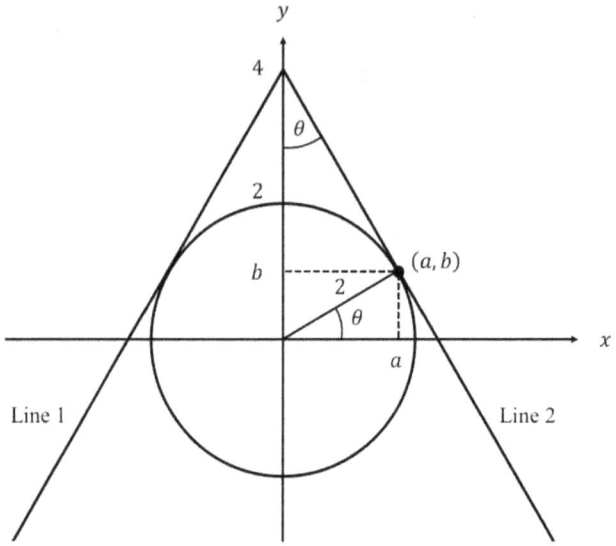

To find the coordinates (a, b), first find the angle θ by considering the larger triangle:

$$\sin \theta = \frac{2}{4} = \frac{1}{2}$$

$$\theta = 30°$$

Now consider the smaller triangle:

$$\sin \theta = \frac{b}{2}$$

$$b = 1$$

a can now be found using Pythagoras' Theorem:

$$a^2 + b^2 = 2^2$$

$$a = \sqrt{4-1} = \sqrt{3}$$

Now the gradient of line 2 can be determined:

$$m_2 = \frac{b-4}{a-0} = \frac{-3}{\sqrt{3}} = -\sqrt{3}$$

As the two lines are symmetrical about the y-axis, $m_1 = -m_2 = \sqrt{3}$. As the y intercept of both lines is 4, their equations are

$$y_1 = \sqrt{3}x + 4 \text{ and } y_2 = -\sqrt{3}x + 4$$

Question 4

i)

$$\log_2 \sqrt[3]{x} = \frac{1}{2}$$

$$\sqrt[3]{x} = 2^{\frac{1}{2}}$$

$$x = \left(2^{\frac{1}{2}}\right)^3 = 2^{\frac{3}{2}} = 2\sqrt{2}$$

ii)

$$\sqrt{\log_8 16} = \sqrt{\log_8 \left(8^{\frac{4}{3}}\right)} = \sqrt{\frac{4}{3}} = \frac{2}{\sqrt{3}}$$

Question 5

We can introduce a substitute variable $y = x^2$:

$$y^2 - 13y + 36 = 0$$
$$(y-9)(y-4) = 0$$
$$y = 9 \text{ or } y = 4$$
$$x^2 = 9 \text{ or } x^2 = 4$$
$$x = \pm 2 \text{ or } \pm 3$$

Question 6

The right-hand side of the inequality is a geometric series with first term 1 and common ratio $\frac{1}{x}$. The sum to infinity is then

$$S_\infty = \frac{a}{1-r} = \frac{1}{1-\frac{1}{x}} = \frac{x}{x-1}$$

The inequality then becomes:

$$x + 2 < \frac{x}{x-1}$$

Multiply each side by $(x-1)^2$ (as it is always positive, the inequality stays the same):

$$(x+2)(x-1)^2 < x(x-1)$$
$$x^3 - 3x + 2 < x^2 - x$$
$$x^3 - x^2 - 2x + 2 < 0$$
$$(x-1)(x^2 - 2) < 0$$

$$(x-1)(x+\sqrt{2})(x-\sqrt{2}) < 0$$

For the overall inequality to be satisfied, either all three brackets must be positive, or two brackets must be negative and one bracket must be positive. Consider each bracket on a number line:

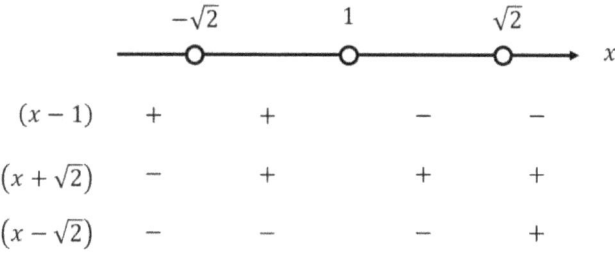

Given also that $x > 0$,

$$1 < x < \sqrt{2}$$

Question 7

There are 6 possible combinations that give a total of 10 or higher: $(4,6)$, $(6,4)$, $(5,5)$, $(5,6)$, $(6,5)$ and $(6,6)$. Each has a probability of $\frac{1}{36}$ of occurring. Hence, the total probability is $6 \times \frac{1}{36} = \frac{1}{6}$.

If the sum of the first two dice is at least 10, then there are three possible values that the sum can be: 10, 11 and 12, and six possible combinations that give these values, as listed above. Consider each possible sum in turn.

The combinations that give a total of 10 are $(4,6)$, $(6,4)$ and $(5,5)$, so there is a total probability of $\frac{3}{6}$ of this occurring. A 5 or a 6 is then required to reach a total of 15, so this gives an overall probability of $\frac{3}{6} \times \frac{2}{6} = \frac{6}{36}$.

The combinations that give a total of 11 are $(5,6)$ and $(6,5)$, so there is a total probability of $\frac{2}{6}$ of this occurring. A 4, 5 or 6 is then required to reach a total of 15, so this gives an overall probability of $\frac{2}{6} \times \frac{3}{6} = \frac{6}{36}$.

Finally, the combination that gives a total of 12 is $(6,6)$, which has a probability of $\frac{1}{6}$ of occurring. A 3, 4, 5 or 6 is then required to reach a total of 15, so this gives an overall probability of $\frac{1}{6} \times \frac{4}{6} = \frac{4}{36}$.

The total probability is therefore

$$\frac{6}{36} + \frac{6}{36} + \frac{4}{36} = \frac{16}{36} = \frac{4}{9}$$

Question 8

The easiest way to obtain a sketch of the function is to use the double angle formula for $\cos 2x$:

$$\cos 2x = \cos^2 x - \sin^2 x = 1 - 2\sin^2 x$$

The sketch of $y = \cos 2x$ can then be obtained by scaling the graph of $y = \cos x$ by a factor $\frac{1}{2}$ in the x direction.

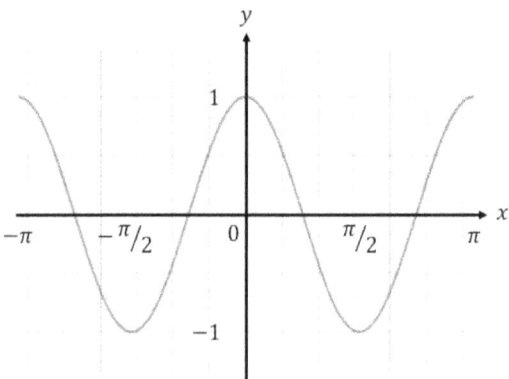

Alternatively, it is possible to obtain this sketch by starting with the graph of $y = \sin x$ and then squaring it, scaling by a factor of 2 in the y direction, reflecting in the x-axis and then shifting up the y-axis by 1.

Question 9

First, we need to find the limits of the area, when $y = 0$:

$$y = \frac{(x^2 - 4x)}{\sqrt{x}} = 0$$

$$x^2 - 4x = 0$$

$$x(x - 4) = 0$$

$$x = 0 \text{ and } x = 4$$

Integrating a function gives the area under the curve, so in this case the negative of the integral is required:

$$A = -\int_0^4 \left(\frac{x^2 - 4x}{\sqrt{x}}\right) dx = -\int_0^4 \left(x^{\frac{3}{2}} - 4x^{\frac{1}{2}}\right) dx = -\left[\frac{2}{5}x^{\frac{5}{2}} - \frac{8}{3}x^{\frac{3}{2}}\right]_0^4$$

$$A = -\left(\frac{2}{5}(4)^{\frac{5}{2}} - \frac{8}{3}(4)^{\frac{3}{2}}\right) = \frac{8}{3}(\sqrt{4})^3 - \frac{2}{5}(\sqrt{4})^5$$

$$A = \frac{8}{3} \times 8 - \frac{2}{5} \times 32 = \frac{64}{3} - \frac{64}{5} = 64\left(\frac{5}{15} - \frac{3}{15}\right) = \frac{128}{15}$$

Question 10

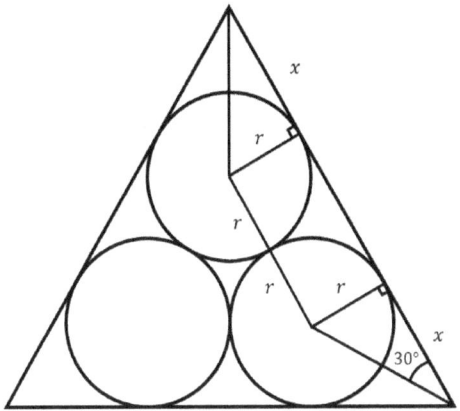

By considering the triangle with angle 30° labelled,

$$\tan 30 = \frac{r}{x}$$

$$x = \sqrt{3}r$$

The side length of the triangle is therefore

$$L = x + 2r + x = (2 + 2\sqrt{3})r$$

The area of the triangle is

$$A_t = \frac{1}{2}L^2 \sin 60 = \frac{1}{2}(2 + 2\sqrt{3})^2 r^2 \frac{\sqrt{3}}{2}$$

$$A_t = \frac{\sqrt{3}}{4}(16 + 8\sqrt{3})r^2 = (4\sqrt{3} + 6)r^2$$

$$\therefore \frac{A_{circles}}{A_{triangle}} = \frac{3\pi r^2}{(4\sqrt{3} + 6)r^2} = \frac{3\pi}{(4\sqrt{3} + 6)}$$

Question 11

If the sequence is an arithmetic progression, then there must be a common difference between each term. Hence,

$$a - \frac{a}{b} = \frac{a}{b} - \left(-\frac{a}{b}\right)$$

$$a\left(\frac{b-1}{b}\right) = \frac{2a}{b}$$

$$b - 1 = 2$$

$$b = 3$$

Question 12

Use a binomial expansion:

$$(2.1)^5 = (2 + 0.1)^5$$

$$= 2^5 + 5(2)^4(0.1) + 10(2)^3(0.1)^2 + 10(2)^2(0.1)^3 + \cdots$$

$$= 32 + 8 + 0.8 + 0.04 = \mathbf{40.8}$$

END OF SECTION

PART B

Question 13: A

Consider mass-energy conservation per second:

$$E = mc^2 = 3.8 \times 10^{26} \text{ J}$$

$$m = \frac{3.8 \times 10^{26}}{(3 \times 10^8)^2} = \frac{3.8}{9} \times 10^{10} = \mathbf{4.2 \times 10^9 \text{ kg}}$$

Question 14: C

As the batteries are connected in parallel, the **maximum voltage stays the same**. However, the current from each will be added and so **maximum current is higher**.

Question 15: C

A total solar eclipse cannot be seen since the angular diameter of the Sun is larger than the angular diameter of Titan, as seen from the surface of Saturn. This means that Titan can never completely block the Sun and cause a total solar eclipse.

PAT PAST PAPER SOLUTIONS 2009

Question 16: C

Initially, the combined boat and anchor float on the lake, so Archimedes' principle gives $(M + m)g = V_d \rho_w g$, where M and m are the masses of the boat and anchor respectively, V_d is the volume of water displaced and ρ_w is the density of the water. This can be rearranged to get

$$V_d = \frac{M + m}{\rho_w} = \frac{M}{\rho_w} + \frac{m}{\rho_w}$$

After the anchor is dropped, the total displaced volume consists of volume displaced by the boat and volume displaced by the anchor. The volume displaced by the boat is $\frac{M}{\rho_w}$, and the volume displaced by the anchor is equal to the anchor volume, as it is fully submerged. Hence, the final displaced volume is $V_d' = \frac{M}{\rho_w} + V_a = \frac{M}{\rho_w} + \frac{m}{\rho_a}$, where V_a and ρ_a are the volume and density of the anchor.

As $\rho_a > \rho_w$, then $V_d' < V_d$. This means that the displaced volume of water after dropping the anchor is smaller than the initial displaced volume, and so the water level **falls slightly**.

Question 17: B

Assuming all gravitational potential energy is converted into thermal energy,

$$mgh = mc\Delta T$$

$$\Delta T = \frac{gh}{c} = \frac{10 \times 105}{4.2 \times 10^3} = \frac{1.05 \times 10^3}{4.2 \times 10^3} = \mathbf{0.25°C}$$

PAT PAST PAPER SOLUTIONS 2009

Question 18: D

Rearrange the equation to make m the subject and substitute in the values given in the question:

$$t = d\sqrt{\frac{m}{2qU}}$$

$$m = 2qU\left(\frac{t}{d}\right)^2 = 2 \times 1.6 \times 10^{-19} \times 16 \times 10^3 \times \left(\frac{30 \times 10^{-6}}{1.5}\right)^2$$

$$m = 2 \times 1.6^2 \times 10^{-16} \times (2 \times 10^{-5})^2 = 8 \times 2.56 \times 10^{-26}$$

$$m \approx 20 \times 10^{-26} = \mathbf{2 \times 10^{-24} \ kg}$$

Question 19: D

$$K = \frac{F}{v^2 A} = \frac{[\text{kgms}^{-2}]}{[\text{ms}^{-1}]^2[\text{m}^2]} = \frac{[\text{kgms}^{-2}]}{[\text{m}^4\text{s}^{-2}]} = [\text{kgm}^{-3}]$$

K is therefore a **density**.

Question 20: C

Initially, the current increases due to the decrease in resistance. As the capacitor then charges, the current gradually decreases.

Question 21: B

As light is moving into a denser medium, refraction will cause it to bend towards the normal and hence travel down.

Question 22: A

Centripetal acceleration is given by

$$a = \omega^2 r = \left(\frac{2\pi}{T}\right)^2 r = \left(\frac{2\pi}{2.4 \times 10^6}\right)^2 \times 4 \times 10^8$$

$$a = \frac{4 \times 4 \times \pi^2}{2.4^2} \times 10^{-4} \approx \frac{16 \times 10}{6} \times 10^{-4} = 2.7 \times 10^{-3} \text{ ms}^{-2}$$

Question 23

Rearrange the equation to make A the subject and then substitute in the values given in the question:

$$A = \frac{P}{kT^4} = \frac{75}{(6 \times 10^{-8}) \times 5000^4} = \frac{75}{6 \times 625} \times \frac{1}{10^{-8} \times 10^{12}}$$

$$A = \frac{1}{50} \times 10^{-4} = 2 \times 10^{-6} \text{ m}^2$$

PAT PAST PAPER SOLUTIONS 2009

Question 24

Let p, q and r be the lengths of pangs, quizzers and roodles, respectively. Then:

$$q + r = 2p$$
$$q = 2p - r \quad (1)$$
$$q^2 = 2p^2 + r^2 \quad (2)$$

Substitute (1) into (2):

$$(2p - r)^2 = 2p^2 + r^2$$
$$4p^2 - 4pr + r^2 = 2p^2 + r^2$$
$$2p^2 = 4pr$$
$$p = 2r \quad (3)$$

Substitute (3) into (1):

$$q = 2(2r) - r$$
$$q = 3r \quad (4)$$

Let $q^3 = ap^3 + br^3$, where a and b are the number of pangs and roodles used, respectively. Substitute in (3) and (4):

$$(3r)^3 = a(2r)^3 + br^3$$
$$27r^3 = 8ar^3 + br^3$$
$$27 = 8a + b$$
$$b = 27 - 8a \quad (5)$$

To minimise the required number of crew required, $ap^2 + br^2$ must be minimised:

$$ap^2 + br^2 = (4a + b)r^2$$

Therefore $(4a + b)$ needs to be minimised. Possible values of a and b are shown in the table below:

a	b (from (5))	$4a + b$
1	19	23
2	11	19
3	3	15

Therefore the optimal combination is **3 pangs and 3 roodles**.

Question 25

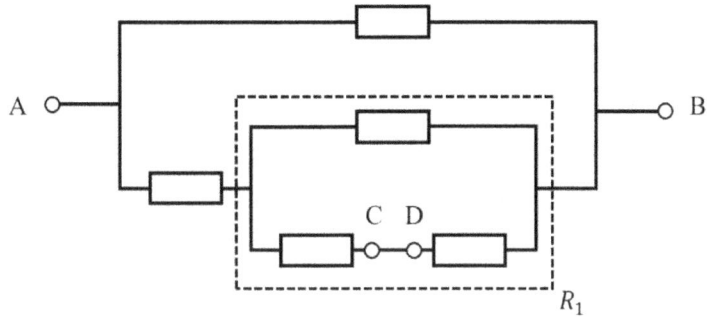

The resistance of block R_1 is given by

$$\frac{1}{R_1} = \frac{1}{1} + \frac{1}{2} = \frac{3}{2}$$

$$R_1 = \frac{2}{3} \text{ k}\Omega$$

The resistance across the bottom line of resistors is

$$R_{bottom} = 1 + \frac{2}{3} = \frac{5}{3} \text{ k}\Omega$$

The overall resistance from A to B is therefore

$$\frac{1}{R_{AB}} = \frac{1}{R_{top}} + \frac{1}{R_{bottom}} = \frac{1}{1} + \frac{3}{5} = \frac{8}{5}$$

$$R_{AB} = \frac{5}{8} \text{ k}\Omega = \mathbf{625\ \Omega}$$

Taking into account internal resistance, the voltage between terminals A and B is given by

$$V_{AB} = 6 \times \frac{R_{AB}}{R_{AB} + r} = 6 \times \frac{625}{625 + 125} = 6 \times \frac{5}{6} = \mathbf{5\ V}$$

As the top and bottom lines are in parallel, the voltage across the bottom line will also be equal to 5 V. The voltage across the resistor block R_1 is

$$V_1 = 5 \times \frac{R_1}{R_1 + 1} = 5 \times \frac{2/3}{2/3 + 1} = 5 \times \frac{2/3}{5/3} = 2\text{ V}$$

The voltage across the bottom line of R_1 is therefore also equal to 2 V, and so the current in the wire connecting C and D is

$$I_{CD} = \frac{2}{2 \times 10^3} = 1\text{ mA}$$

Question 26

The electron gains kinetic energy from electrical potential energy due to the potential difference:

$$\frac{1}{2}mv^2 = eV$$

$$v^2 = \frac{2eV}{m} = \frac{2 \times 1.6 \times 10^{-19} \times 50}{10^{-30}} = 16 \times 10^{12}$$

$$v = 4 \times 10^6 \text{ ms}^{-1}$$

This is the horizontal speed of the electron as it leaves the electron gun. The time taken to reach the screen is therefore

$$t = \frac{0.4}{4 \times 10^6} = 10^{-7}\text{ s}$$

Taking downwards as positive, the vertical displacement during this period is given by

$$s = ut + \frac{1}{2}at^2 = \frac{1}{2} \times 10 \times (10^{-7})^2 = 5 \times 10^{-14}\text{ m}$$

Question 27

i) The energy dispersed by the brakes must be equal to the kinetic energy of the car:

$$E_{brakes} = \frac{1}{2}mv^2$$

ii) The time between subsequent stops is $t = \frac{s}{v}$, so the average power dissipated is

$$P = \frac{E_{brakes}}{t} = \frac{1}{2}mv^2 \times \frac{v}{s} = \frac{mv^3}{2s}$$

iii) The total time taken to travel a distance d is $t = \frac{d}{v}$. The energy required is therefore

$$E = Pt = P \times \frac{d}{v} = \frac{mv^3}{2s} \times \frac{d}{v} = \frac{mv^2 d}{2s}$$

iv) Using the values given in the question,

$$E = \frac{1000 \times 10^2 \times 1000}{2 \times 100} = 5 \times 10^5 \text{ J}$$

Since $E \propto v^2$, if the speed is doubled

$$E_2 = 2^2 \times E_1 = 2 \times 10^6 \text{ J}$$

v) In a time t, the car will travel a distance vt. Hence the volume of air swept out is

$$V = Avt$$

The kinetic energy transferred to this volume of air during time t is therefore

$$E_{air} = \frac{1}{2}mv^2 = \frac{1}{2}(DV)v^2 = \frac{1}{2}ADv^3 t$$

The power required is therefore

$$P = \frac{E_{air}}{t} = \frac{1}{2}ADv^3$$

vi) The time taken to travel 1 km is $t = \frac{1000}{10} = 100$ s. The total energy used is equal to the sum of the energy transferred to the air plus the energy required by the car to move:

$$E_{tot} = E_{air} + E$$

Substituting the value of E for 1 km from part (d) and using the formula derived in part (e),

$$E_{tot} = \frac{1}{2}ADv^3 t + 5 \times 10^5$$

$$E_{tot} = \frac{1}{2} \times 1 \times 1 \times 10^3 \times 100 + 5 \times 10^5 = 5 \times 10^4 + 5 \times 10^5$$

$$E_{tot} = 5.5 \times 10^5 \text{ J}$$

vii) The distance between stops, s, is given by $s = vt$, where t is the time between stops.

$$E_{brakes} = E_{air}$$

$$\frac{1}{2}mv^2 = \frac{1}{2}ADv^3 t = \frac{1}{2}ADsv^2$$

$$s = \frac{m}{AD} = \frac{1000}{1 \times 1} = \mathbf{1\ km}$$

viii) On highways, s will be large and so more energy is lost to air resistance. Hence a smaller area (A) should be prioritised.

In cities, s is small and so more energy is lost to braking. Hence a lighter design (smaller m) should be prioritised.

END OF PAPER

2010

PART A

Question 1

i)

$$\sin 3x = \sqrt{3} \cos 3x$$

$$\tan 3x = \sqrt{3}$$

$$3x = \frac{\pi}{3}, \frac{4\pi}{3}, \frac{7\pi}{3}$$

$$x = \frac{\pi}{9}, \frac{4\pi}{9}, \frac{7\pi}{9}$$

ii) Use the identity $\sin^2 x + \cos^2 x = 1$:

$$\cos^2 x - \sin x + 1 = 0$$

$$(1 - \sin^2 x) - \sin x + 1 = 0$$

$$\sin^2 x + \sin x - 2 = 0$$

$$(\sin x + 2)(\sin x - 1) = 0$$

$$\sin x \neq -2 \text{ so } \sin x = 1$$

$$x = \frac{\pi}{2}$$

Question 2

The larger circle has centre $(1, 1)$ and radius 1 as shown in the diagram.

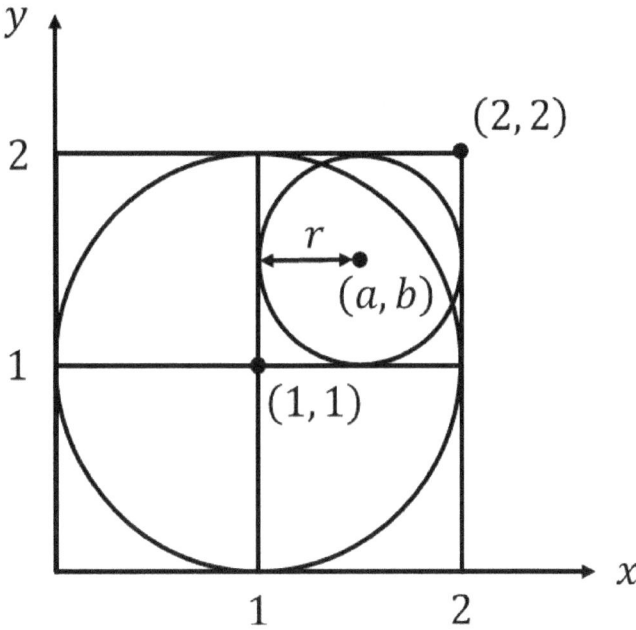

The diameter of the smaller circle is equal to the radius of the larger circle, hence $r = \frac{1}{2}$. It is also clear from the diagram that the centre of the smaller circle is the midpoint of the line between $(1, 1)$ and $(2, 2)$, which is therefore $\left(\frac{3}{2}, \frac{3}{2}\right)$. Hence, the equation of the smaller circle is

$$\left(x - \frac{3}{2}\right)^2 + \left(y - \frac{3}{2}\right)^2 = \frac{1}{4}$$

Question 3

Let $f(x) = x^3 + 2x^2 - 5x - 6$.

$$f(-1) = (-1)^3 + 2(-1)^2 - 5(-1) - 6 = -1 + 2 + 5 - 6 = 0$$

$$\therefore x = -1 \text{ is a root}$$

One of the factors of $f(x)$ must therefore be $(x + 1)$:

$$x^3 + 2x^2 - 5x - 6 = 0$$

$$(x + 1)(x^2 + x - 6) = 0$$

$$(x + 1)(x + 3)(x - 2) = 0$$

The other two roots are therefore

$$x = 2, x = -3$$

Question 4

The gradient of the line is

$$m = \frac{y_2 - y_1}{x_2 - x_1} = \frac{5 - 3}{1 - 2} = -2$$

The equation of the line is therefore

$$y - y_1 = m(x - x_1)$$

$$y - 3 = -2(x - 2)$$

$$y - 3 = -2x + 4$$

$$y = -2x + 7$$

Question 5

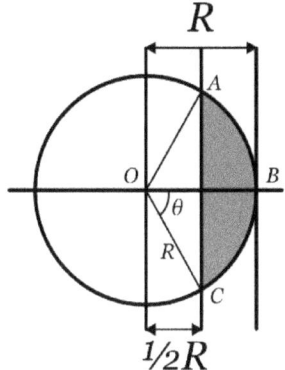

Consider the triangle with angle θ labelled:

$$\cos \theta = \frac{{}^{1}\!/_{2} R}{R} = \frac{1}{2}$$

$$\theta = 60°$$

The area of the sector OABC is

$$A_{OABC} = \frac{2 \times 60}{360} \pi R^2 = \frac{\pi R^2}{3}$$

The area of the triangle OAC is

$$A_{OAC} = \frac{1}{2} R^2 \sin 120 = \frac{\sqrt{3} R^2}{4}$$

The shaded area is therefore

$$A_s = A_{OABC} - A_{OAC} = \frac{\pi R^2}{3} - \frac{\sqrt{3} R^2}{4} = R^2 \left(\frac{\pi}{3} - \frac{\sqrt{3}}{4} \right)$$

Question 6

Let one side of the rectangle of length x, and the other have length y. The perimeter is therefore equal to the length of wire:

$$2x + 2y = L$$

$$y = \frac{L}{2} - x$$

The area is then given by

$$A = xy = x\left(\frac{L}{2} - x\right) = \frac{L}{2}x - x^2$$

To maximise area, differentiate with respect to x and set to zero:

$$\frac{dA}{dx} = \frac{L}{2} - 2x = 0$$

$$x = \frac{L}{4}$$

$$A = \frac{L}{4}\left(\frac{L}{2} - \frac{L}{4}\right) = \frac{L^2}{16}$$

Question 7

i) Apply the definition of a log:

$$\log_3 9 = 2$$

ii) Change the number inside each log to have base 2:

$$\log 4 + \log 16 - \log 2 = \log(2^2) + \log(2^4) - \log 2$$
$$= 2\log 2 + 4\log 2 - \log 2 = 5\log 2$$

Alternatively, using addition and subtraction laws of logs:

$$\log 4 + \log 16 - \log 2 = \log\left(\frac{4 \times 16}{2}\right) = \log 32 = \log(2^5) = 5\log 2$$

Question 8

i) Expand the addition inside the bracket and then expand the bracket:

$$(16.1)^2 = (16 + 0.1)^2 = 16^2 + 2(16)(0.1) + 0.1^2$$
$$= 256 + 3.2 + 0.01 = \mathbf{259.21}$$

ii) Again expand each term:

$$10.11 \times 3.2 = (10 + 0.11)(3 + 0.2) = 30 + 2 + 0.33 + 0.022$$
$$= \mathbf{32.352}$$

Question 9

$$u_1 = x^3, u_4 = x, u_7 = x^2$$

An arithmetic progression must have a common difference, d, between each term. Hence there is a difference $3d$ between the first and fourth terms, and the same difference between the fourth and seventh terms. Consider the difference between u_1 and u_4, and also between u_1 and u_7:

$$x = x^3 + 3d$$

$$2x = 2x^3 + 6d \quad (1)$$

$$x^2 = x^3 + 6d \quad (2)$$

$(1) - (2)$:

$$2x - x^2 = 2x^3 - x^3 + 6d - 6d$$

$$x^3 + x^2 - 2x = 0$$

$$x(x^2 + x - 2) = 0$$

$$x(x + 2)(x - 1) = 0$$

$$\therefore x = 0 \text{ or } -2 \text{ or } 1$$

But, $x \neq 0$ and $x \neq 1$:

$$x = -2$$

$$d = \frac{x - x^3}{3} = \frac{(-2) - (-2)^3}{3} = \frac{-2 + 8}{3} = 2$$

Question 10

To obtain an even number of points, either the first roll must be a 2 or 4, or the first roll must be a 6 and the second roll a 2, 4 or 6. The probability of obtaining any specific number on a given roll is $\frac{1}{6}$, so the probability of initially obtaining a 2 or a 4 is $\frac{1}{6} + \frac{1}{6} = \frac{1}{3}$. The probability of obtaining a 6 and then an even number is equal to the individual probabilities multiplied together:

$$P(6, \text{even}) = \frac{1}{6} \times \frac{3}{6} = \frac{1}{12}$$

The total probability of obtaining an even number of points is therefore

$$\frac{1}{3} + \frac{1}{12} = \frac{4+1}{12} = \mathbf{\frac{5}{12}}$$

Question 11

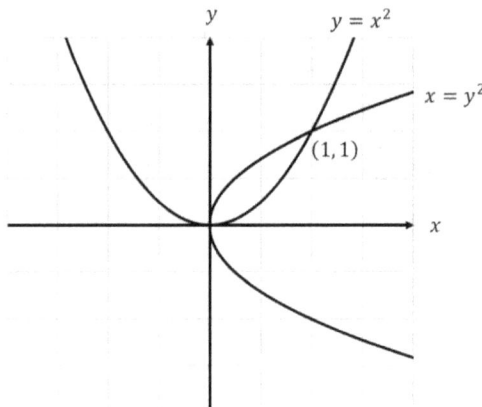

To find the points of intersection, substitute $x = y^2$ into $y = x^2$:

$$y = y^4$$

$$y = 0 \text{ or } y = 1$$

Hence the points of intersection are $(0, 0)$ and $(1, 1)$.

The area between the curves is equal to the area between $x = y^2$ and the x-axis minus the area between $y = x^2$ and the x-axis. $x = y^2$ can be written as $y = \pm\sqrt{x}$, and since the curve is only relevant to finding the area for the section above the x-axis, it can be written as $y = \sqrt{x}$. Hence, integrate to find the area as described:

$$A = \int_0^1 \left(\sqrt{x} - x^2\right) dx = \int_0^1 \left(x^{\frac{1}{2}} - x^2\right) dx$$

$$A = \left[\frac{2}{3}x^{\frac{3}{2}} - \frac{x^3}{3}\right]_0^1 = \frac{2}{3} - \frac{1}{3} = \frac{1}{3}$$

END OF SECTION

PART B

Question 12: B

After 16000 years, two half-lives will have passed for element A, and so there will be $\frac{1}{2} \times \frac{1}{2} = \frac{1}{4}$ of the initial amount remaining. Element B will have experienced exactly one half-life, so there will be $\frac{1}{2}$ of the initial amount remaining. Hence,

$$\text{A:B} = \frac{1}{4} : \frac{1}{2} = \mathbf{1:2}$$

Question 13: A

The voltage across resistor R_1 is given by the potential divider equation: $V_1 = \frac{R_1}{R_1+R_2} V$. The power dissipated by the resistor is then

$$P_1 = \frac{V_1^2}{R_1} = \frac{\left(\frac{R_1}{R_1+R_2}V\right)^2}{R_1} = \frac{\mathbf{V^2 R_1}}{\mathbf{(R_1+R_2)^2}}$$

Question 14: C

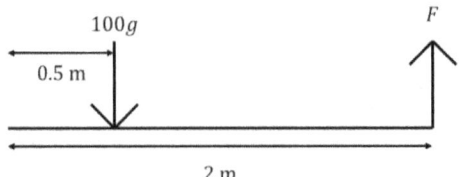

For the builder to lift the block, the total moment about the pivot (the other end of the plank) must be zero:

$$2 \times F = 100 \times 10 \times 0.5$$

$$F = \frac{1000}{4} = 250 \text{ N}$$

Question 15: B

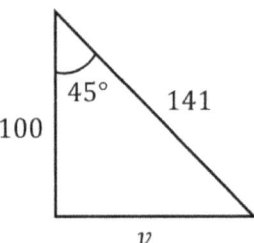

The diagram of the velocities is as above. By inspection, this is a right-angled triangle, as $141 \approx 100\sqrt{2}$ and $\cos 45 = \frac{1}{\sqrt{2}} = \frac{100}{100\sqrt{2}}$. Therefore,

$$v^2 = \left(100\sqrt{2}\right)^2 - 100^2 = 10000 \times 2 - 10000 = 10000$$

$$v = 100 \text{ km/hr}$$

As shown on the diagram, the actual speed relative to the ground is **west**.

PAT PAST PAPER SOLUTIONS | 2010

Question 16: A

$$\lambda = \frac{c}{f} = \frac{3 \times 10^8}{1000 \times 1000} = \mathbf{300\ m}$$

Question 17: B

The diagram of the incident light can be drawn as follows:

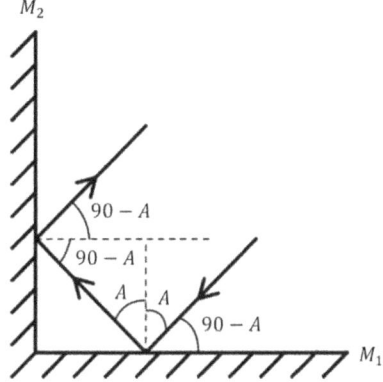

From this diagram, the resultant beam is clearly at an angle of **180°** to the incident beam.

Question 18: C

$$Q = CV = (3 \times 10^{-9}) \times (10) = \mathbf{3 \times 10^{-8}\ C}$$

Question 19: B

$$x = \frac{F}{k} = \frac{mg}{k} = \frac{80 \times 10}{80000} = 0.01\ \text{m} = \mathbf{10\ mm}$$

Question 20: C

From Kepler's 2nd Law,

$$v_1 r_1 = v_2 r_2$$

$$(50)(4 \times 10^{10}) = v_2 (10 \times 10^{10})$$

$$v_2 = 20 \text{ km/s}$$

Question 21: D

Consider the diagram below, where h_2 is the true depth of the fish and h_1 is the apparent depth:

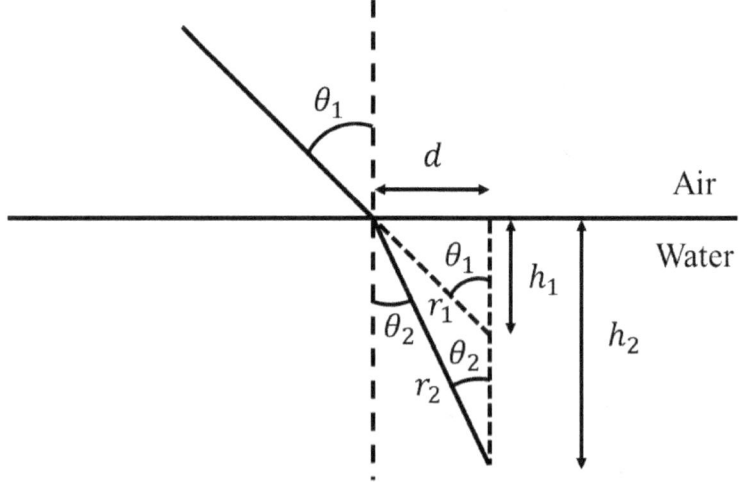

Using Snell's law,

$$n_1 \sin \theta_1 = n_2 \sin \theta_2$$

$$\frac{\sin \theta_1}{\sin \theta_2} = \frac{n_2}{n_1} = \frac{1.33}{1} = \frac{4}{3}$$

PAT PAST PAPER SOLUTIONS 2010

Considering the triangles in the diagram above,

$$r_1 \sin \theta_1 = d = r_2 \sin \theta_2$$

$$\frac{r_2}{r_1} = \frac{\sin \theta_1}{\sin \theta_2} = \frac{4}{3}$$

$h_1 = r_1 \cos \theta_1$ and $h_2 = r_2 \cos \theta_2$ and so

$$\frac{h_2}{h_1} = \frac{r_2 \cos \theta_2}{r_1 \cos \theta_1} = \frac{4 \cos \theta_2}{3 \cos \theta_1}$$

Since $\theta_1 > \theta_2$, $\cos \theta_1 < \cos \theta_2$ and so

$$\frac{h_2}{h_1} > \frac{4}{3}$$

$$h_2 > \frac{4}{3} \times 0.75$$

$$\boldsymbol{h_2 > 1 \text{ m}}$$

Question 22

The observations can be written mathematically as:

A) $r = b + g \rightarrow g = r - b$ (1)

B) $g^2 = 4b^2 \rightarrow g = 2b$ (2)

D) $\rho b^3 = 3 \rightarrow b^3 = \dfrac{3}{\rho}$ (3)

Substitute (1) into (2):

$$r - b = 2b$$

$$b = \frac{r}{3} \quad (4)$$

Now substitute (4) into (3):

$$\left(\frac{r}{3}\right)^3 = \frac{3}{\rho}$$

$$r^3 = \frac{81}{\rho}$$

$$m_r = \rho r^3 = \mathbf{81\,g}$$

Substitute (2) into (3):

$$\left(\frac{g}{2}\right)^3 = \frac{3}{\rho}$$

$$g^3 = \frac{24}{\rho}$$

$$m_g = \rho g^3 = \mathbf{24\,g}$$

Since the volume of water displaced by the green duck is equal to the volume of the green duck itself,

$$V_d = \frac{32}{1000} = \frac{m_g}{\rho}$$

$$\rho = \frac{1000 \times 24}{32} = 1000 \times \frac{3}{4} = 750 \text{ kgm}^{-3}$$

Question 23

The energy is absorbed by the frying pan as thermal energy, so

$$E = \bar{P}At = m_p c_p \Delta T$$

The time taken to reach a temperature of 70°C is therefore

$$t = \frac{m_p c_p \Delta T}{\bar{P}A} = \frac{2 \times 490 \times (70 - 20)}{10^3 \times 0.07} = \frac{49 \times 10^3}{7 \times 10} = 700 \text{ s}$$

The final temperature of the water will be reached when both the frying pan and the water are at the same temperature, T_f:

$$m_s c_s (70 - T_f) = m_w c_w (T_f - 20)$$

$$2 \times 490 \times (70 - T_f) = 4 \times 4200 \times (T_f - 20)$$

$$4.9 \times 10^2 \times (70 - T_f) = 2 \times 4.2 \times 10^3 \times (T_f - 20)$$

$$7(70 - T_f) = 120(T_f - 20)$$

$$490 + 2400 = T_f(120 + 7)$$

$$T_f = \frac{2890}{127} = 22.8°C$$

Question 24

Based on the information in the question, the system is as follows:

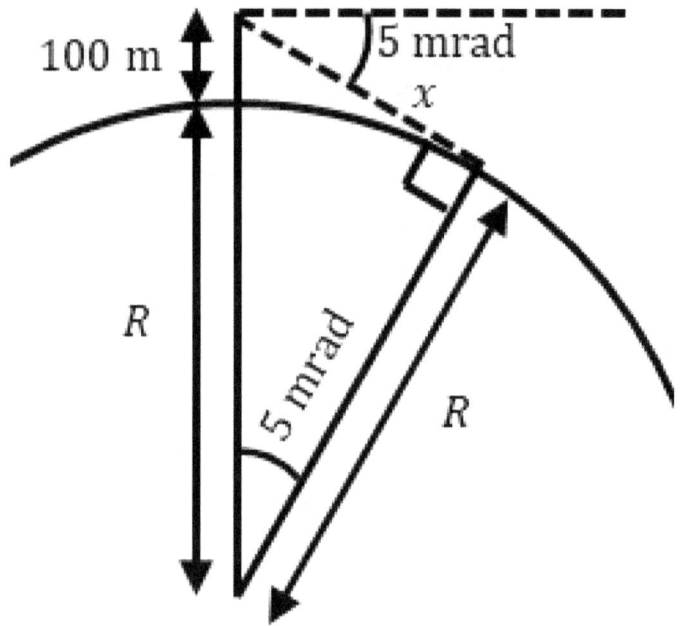

Using the larger triangle formed, $\cos(5 \times 10^{-3}) = \frac{R}{R+100}$. Since, for small angles, $\cos\theta \approx 1 - \frac{\theta^2}{2}$,

$$1 - \frac{(5 \times 10^{-3})^2}{2} = \frac{R}{R+100}$$

$$(2 - 25 \times 10^{-6})(R + 100) = 2R$$

$$2R - 25R \times 10^{-6} + 200 - 25 \times 10^{-4} = 2R$$

$$R = \frac{200 - 25 \times 10^{-4}}{25 \times 10^{-6}} \approx \frac{200}{25 \times 10^{-6}} = \mathbf{8 \times 10^6 \text{ m}}$$

To find the distance of from the astronaut to the horizon, x, use Pythagoras' theorem on the same triangle:

$$(R + 100)^2 = x^2 + R^2$$

$$R^2 + 200R + 10^4 = x^2 + R^2$$

$$x^2 = 200R + 10^4 = 200 \times 8 \times 10^6 + 10^4 \approx 16 \times 10^8$$

$$x = \mathbf{4 \times 10^4 \text{ m}}$$

Question 25

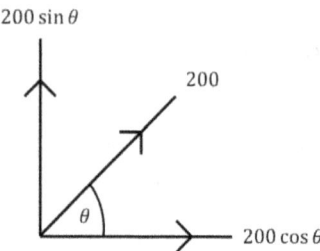

In order for the projectile to land in the rail car, the horizontal component of the projectile's velocity must be equal to the velocity of the rail car:

$$200 \cos \theta = 100$$

$$\cos \theta = \frac{1}{2}$$

$$\theta = 60°$$

At maximum altitude, the vertical velocity of the projectile is zero. Taking upwards as positive,

$$v = u + at$$

$$0 = 200 \sin 60 - 10 \times t$$

$$t = 20 \times \frac{\sqrt{3}}{2} = 10\sqrt{3} \approx 10 \times 1.732 = \mathbf{17.3 \text{ s}}$$

Since the motion of the projectile is symmetrical, the time taken for it to land will be twice the time taken for it to reach maximum height. Since there is no horizontal acceleration,

$$s = ut + \frac{1}{2}at^2 = 200 \cos 60 \times 2 \times 17.3$$

$$s = 200 \times 17.3 = \mathbf{3.46\ km}$$

The maximum altitude can be calculated by considering the vertical displacement of the projectile, again taking upwards as positive:

$$h = ut + \frac{1}{2}at^2$$

$$h = 200 \sin 60 \times 10\sqrt{3} - \frac{1}{2} \times 10 \times \left(10\sqrt{3}\right)^2$$

$$h = 100\sqrt{3} \times 10\sqrt{3} - 5 \times 100 \times 3$$

$$h = 3000 - 1500 = \mathbf{1.5\ km}$$

The kinetic energy of the car is constant throughout:

$$KE_{car} = \frac{1}{2}mv^2 = \frac{1}{2} \times 200 \times 100^2 = 10^6\ \text{J} = \mathbf{1\ MJ}$$

The initial kinetic energy of the projectile in the horizontal and vertical directions (x and y) is

$$KE_x = \frac{1}{2}mu_x^2 = \frac{1}{2} \times 10 \times 100^2 = 0.5 \times 10^5 = \mathbf{50\ kJ}$$

$$KE_y = \frac{1}{2}mu_y^2 = \frac{1}{2} \times 10 \times \left(100\sqrt{3}\right)^2 = 1.5 \times 10^5 = \mathbf{150\ kJ}$$

At the projectile's maximum altitude, all kinetic energy will have been converted to gravitational potential energy, given by $GPE = mgh$:

$$KE_y = GPE$$

$$1.5 \times 10^5 = 10 \times 10 \times h$$

$$h = 1.5 \times 10^3 = \mathbf{1.5\ km}$$

As the rail car is only moving horizontally, the vertical component of the projectile's velocity does not affect the car as it is perpendicular to the car's movement. The horizontal component of the projectile's velocity is equal to the horizontal velocity of the car, and so they combine without the velocity of the car being affected.

The combined car and projectile will be moving at a speed of 100 m/s, with a total mass of 210 kg. Their total kinetic energy is therefore

$$KE_{total} = \frac{1}{2}mv^2 = \frac{1}{2} \times 210 \times 100^2$$

$$KE_{total} = \frac{2.1}{2} \times 10^6 = 1.05 \times 10^6 = \mathbf{1.05\ MJ}$$

END OF PAPER

2011

PART A

Question 1

Use the identity $\sin^2\theta + \cos^2\theta = 1$:

$$\sin\theta - 2\cos^2\theta = -1$$
$$\sin\theta - 2(1 - \sin^2\theta) = -1$$
$$2\sin^2\theta + \sin\theta - 1 = 0$$
$$(2\sin\theta - 1)(\sin\theta + 1) = 0$$
$$\sin\theta = \frac{1}{2} \text{ or } \sin\theta = -1$$
$$\theta = \frac{\pi}{6}, \frac{5\pi}{6}, \frac{\pi}{2}$$

Question 2

$$y = 3 + 2\sin\left((x-3)\frac{\pi}{3}\right)$$

The function $\sin x$ ranges from -1 to 1, and so y will have a maximum of $3 + 2 = 5$, and a minimum of $3 - 2 = 1$.

When $x = 0$, $y = 3 + 2\sin(-\pi) = 3$.

$\sin x$ has a minimum at $x = -\frac{\pi}{2}$ and $x = \frac{3\pi}{2}$, so these minima now occur at $x = \left(-\frac{\pi}{2} \times \frac{3}{\pi}\right) + 3 = 1.5$ and similarly at $x = 7.5$.

$\sin x$ also has a maximum when $x = \frac{\pi}{2}$ or $x = \frac{5\pi}{2}$, and so these maxima will now occur at $x = 4.5$ and $x = 10.5$.

The sketch of the function is shown below:

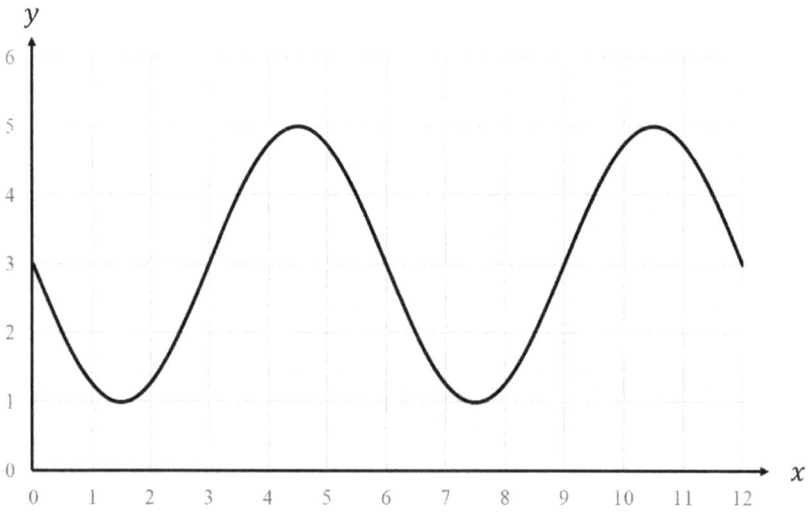

Question 3

As the triangle is equilateral, its internal angles must all be 60°. Also, let the height of the edge of the shaded area be h:

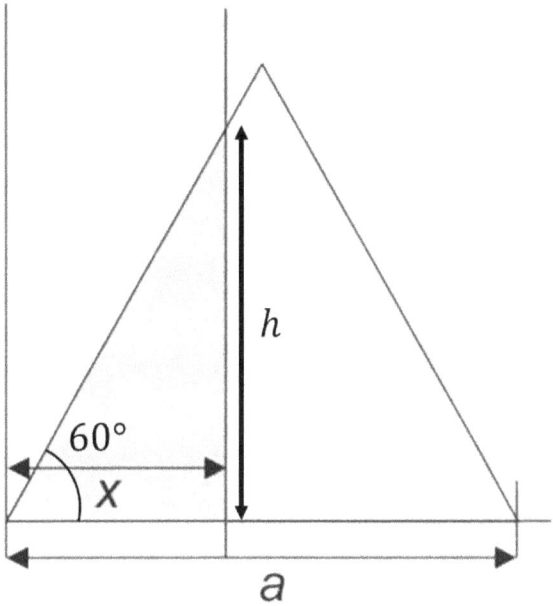

i) For $0 \leq x \leq \frac{a}{2}$, the shaded area lies to the left of the centre of the equilateral triangle, as above.

$$\tan 60 = \frac{h}{x}$$

$$h = \sqrt{3}x$$

$$A = \frac{1}{2}hx = \frac{\sqrt{3}}{2}x^2$$

ii) For $\frac{a}{2} \leq x \leq a$, area A is effectively the unshaded area of the triangle above, which has width $(a-x)$. When $x = \frac{a}{2}$, $h = \frac{\sqrt{3}a}{2}$ and so the area of the larger triangle is

$$\frac{1}{2} \times a \times \frac{\sqrt{3}a}{2} = \frac{\sqrt{3}a^2}{4}$$

Therefore

$$A = \frac{\sqrt{3}a^2}{4} - \frac{\sqrt{3}}{2}(a-x)^2$$

Question 4

Let the radius of the circle be r, and the side of the rhombus be x:

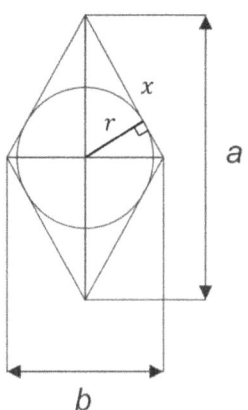

Using similar triangles,

$$\frac{b/2}{r} = \frac{x}{a/2}$$

$$r = \frac{ab}{4x}$$

Since $x^2 = \left(\frac{a}{2}\right)^2 + \left(\frac{b}{2}\right)^2 = \frac{1}{4}(a^2 + b^2)$,

$$A_{circle} = \pi r^2 = \frac{\pi a^2 b^2}{16} \times \frac{4}{a^2 + b^2} = \frac{\pi a^2 b^2}{4(a^2 + b^2)}$$

Since $A_{rhombus} = \frac{1}{2}ab$,

$$\frac{A_{circle}}{A_{rhombus}} = \frac{\pi a^2 b^2}{4(a^2 + b^2)} \times \frac{2}{ab} = \frac{\pi ab}{2(a^2 + b^2)}$$

Question 5

Take logs of both sides and then rearrange:

$$2^x = 10$$

$$\log(2^x) = \log 10$$

$$x \log 2 = \log 10$$

$$x = \frac{\log 10}{\log 2} = \frac{\log 10}{\log 10 - \log 5} \approx \frac{1}{1 - 0.7} = \frac{1}{0.3} \approx 3.3$$

Question 6

Separate the expression into two separate summations, and use the formula for the sum of a geometric series for the first:

$$\sum_{r=1}^{6} \left(2^r + \frac{2r}{3}\right) = \sum_{r=1}^{6} 2^r + \frac{2}{3}\sum_{r=1}^{6} r$$

$$\sum_{r=1}^{6} 2^r = \frac{a(r^n - 1)}{r - 1} = \frac{2(2^6 - 1)}{2 - 1} = 2 \times 63 = 126$$

$$\frac{2}{3}\sum_{r=1}^{6} r = \frac{2}{3}(1 + 2 + 3 + 4 + 5 + 6) = \frac{2}{3} \times 21 = 14$$

$$\therefore \sum_{r=1}^{6} \left(2^r + \frac{2r}{3}\right) = 126 + 14 = 140$$

PAT PAST PAPER SOLUTIONS — 2011

Question 7

Divide the original equation with the known factor $(x^2 - x - 6)$, and then fully factorise:

$$0 = x^4 + 4x^3 - 17x^2 - 24x + 36 = (x^2 - x - 6)(x^2 + 5x - 6)$$

$$0 = (x-3)(x+2)(x+6)(x-1)$$

$$\therefore x = -6, -2, 1, 3$$

Question 8

i) Use partial fractions to split the integral into two parts:

$$\frac{x+2}{(x+1)(x-1)} = \frac{a}{x+1} + \frac{b}{x-1} = \frac{a(x-1) + b(x+1)}{(x+1)(x-1)}$$

Equate the x coefficient and the constant:

$$a + b = 1 \quad (1)$$
$$b - a = 2$$
$$b = a + 2 \quad (2)$$

Substitute (2) into (1):

$$a + a + 2 = 1$$
$$a = -\frac{1}{2}$$

Substitute into (2):

$$b = \frac{3}{2}$$

$$\int \frac{x+2}{(x+1)(x-1)} dx = \frac{1}{2} \int \left(\frac{3}{x-1} - \frac{1}{x+1} \right) dx$$

$$= \frac{3}{2} \int \frac{1}{x-1} dx - \frac{1}{2} \int \frac{1}{x+1} dx$$

$$= \frac{3}{2} \ln(x-1) - \frac{1}{2} \ln(x+1) + \ln A$$

$$= \frac{1}{2} \ln \left(\frac{A(x-1)^3}{x+1} \right)$$

ii)
$$\int_0^1 \frac{1}{\sqrt{x+1}}\,dx = \int_0^1 (x+1)^{-\frac{1}{2}}\,dx$$
$$= \left[2(x+1)^{\frac{1}{2}}\right]_0^1 = 2(\sqrt{2}-1)$$

Question 9

Let $\Delta = y_1 - y_2$. Then

$$\Delta = x^3 - 3x^2 + 2x + 3 - (x^2 - 3x - 4) = x^3 - 4x^2 + 5x + 7$$

To find the maximum and minimum values of Δ, differentiate with respect to x and set to zero:

$$\frac{d\Delta}{dx} = 3x^2 - 8x + 5 = 0$$

$$(3x - 5)(x - 1) = 0$$

$$x = \frac{5}{3} \text{ or } x = 1$$

To identify which point is the maximum and which is the minimum, obtain the second differential at each point.

$$\frac{d^2\Delta}{dx^2} = 6x - 8$$

When $x = \frac{5}{3}$, $\frac{d^2\Delta}{dx^2} = 2 > 0$. Therefore the **minimum** difference occurs at $x = \frac{5}{3}$.

When $x = 1$, $\frac{d^2\Delta}{dx^2} = -2 < 0$. Therefore the **maximum** difference occurs at $x = 1$.

Question 10

Adding and subtracting the two equations gives:

$$s + t = x^2 + y^2 + 2xy = (x+y)^2$$

$$x + y = \pm\sqrt{s+t} \quad (1)$$

$$s - t = x^2 + y^2 - 2xy = (x-y)^2$$

$$x - y = \pm\sqrt{s-t} \quad (2)$$

$(1) + (2)$:

$$2x = \pm\sqrt{s+t} \pm \sqrt{s-t}$$

$$x = \frac{1}{2}\left(\pm\sqrt{s+t} \pm \sqrt{s-t}\right)$$

Rearranging the second equation in the question gives

$$y = \frac{t}{2x} = \frac{t}{\pm\sqrt{s+t} \pm \sqrt{s-t}}$$

Question 11

Since there are $6 \times 6 = 36$ unique combinations of the dice, each must individually map onto a score from 0 to 35.

The maximum score of 35 must occur when both dice show 6:

$$6A + 6B + C = 35 \quad (1)$$

Similarly, the minimum score of 0 must occur when both dice show 1:

$$A + B + C = 0 \quad (2)$$

$6 \times (2) - (1)$:

$$5C = -35$$

$$C = -7$$

Substituting this back into (2) gives

$$A + B - 7 = 0$$

$$A + B = 7 \quad (3)$$

Additionally, consider the second smallest value possible ($S = 1$). This occurs when $d_1 = 1$ and $d_2 = 2$ or vice versa. Considering the first case,

$$A + 2B = 8 \quad (4)$$

$(4) - (3)$:

$$B = 1 \text{ and therefore } A = 6$$

Alternatively, $d_1 = 2$ and $d_2 = 1$ gives $A = 1$ and $B = 6$. Therefore

$$A = 6, B = 1 \text{ and } C = -7 \text{ or } A = 1, B = 6 \text{ and } C = -7$$

END OF SECTION

PART B

Question 12: C

The velocity of the wave is $\frac{45}{25} = \frac{9}{5}$ ms^{-1}. The wavelength is therefore

$$\lambda = \frac{v}{f} = vT = \left(\frac{9}{5}\right)(2) = \mathbf{3.6\ m}$$

Question 13: A

When $T_S = 26°C$, the rate of cooling is

$$\alpha(T_S - T) = 15 \times (26 - 6) = 300\ \text{W}$$

Total power consumption will therefore be

$$\frac{300}{0.3} = 1000\ \text{W} = \mathbf{1\ kW}$$

Question 14: B

A lunar eclipse can only occur when the Earth is exactly aligned in between the sun and the moon. This can therefore only occur when the moon's phase is **full moon**.

Question 15: D

$$\text{Brightness} \propto P_{observed} \propto \frac{P_{radiated}}{r^2}$$

Since the observed power is the same for both stars,

$$\frac{P_d}{r_d^2} = \frac{P_n}{r_n^2}$$

$$\frac{P_d}{P_n} = \left(\frac{r_d}{r_n}\right)^2 = \left(\frac{20}{10}\right)^2 = \mathbf{4.0}$$

Question 16: A

Use Kepler's 3rd law: $T^2 \propto r^3$. Hence,

$$\frac{T_1^2}{r_1^3} = \frac{T_2^2}{r_2^3}$$

$$r_2 = \left(\frac{T_2}{T_1}\right)^{\frac{2}{3}} r_1$$

$$r_2 = \left(\frac{24}{3}\right)^{\frac{2}{3}} (0.4) = 0.4 \times \left(\sqrt[3]{8}\right)^2 = 0.4 \times 4 = \mathbf{1.6\ A.U.}$$

Question 17: D

The resistance of the two resistors in parallel is equal to $\frac{R}{2}$. Hence the resistance of the bottom line is $R + \frac{R}{2} = \frac{3R}{2}$. The overall resistance of the network is therefore

$$\frac{1}{R_T} = \frac{1}{R} + \frac{2}{3R} = \frac{3+2}{3R} = \frac{5}{3R}$$

$$R_T = \frac{3R}{5}$$

Question 18: C

$$\frac{V_1}{V_2} = \frac{N_1}{N_2}$$

$$N_2 = \frac{V_2}{V_1} N_1 = \frac{120}{240} \times 50 = 25$$

PAT PAST PAPER SOLUTIONS — 2011

Question 19: B

The power required to lift the mass is given by $P = Fv$. Equating this to the electrical power gives

$$IV = Fv$$

$$v = \frac{IV}{F} = \frac{IV}{mg} = \frac{1 \times 6}{0.1 \times 10} = \mathbf{6\ ms^{-1}}$$

Question 20: D

The component of the car's weight parallel to the slope is

$$F = mg \sin 30 = ma$$

$$a = g \sin 30 = 10 \times 0.5 = \mathbf{5\ ms^{-2}}$$

Question 21: C

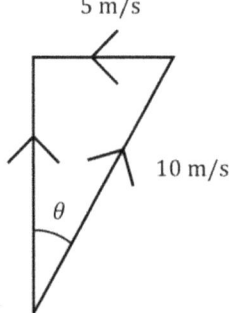

From the triangle above,

$$\sin \theta = \frac{5}{10} = \frac{1}{2}$$

$$\theta = 30°$$

She must therefore steer a course of **30°E**.

Question 22

In the first case, the elastic potential energy is converted into kinetic energy. Hence:

$$\frac{1}{2}k(x-l)^2 = \frac{1}{2}mv^2$$

$$v = \sqrt{\frac{k}{m}}(x-l)$$

In the second case, the elastic potential energy is converted into both kinetic energy and gravitational potential energy. The gravitational energy gained by the ball is equal to mgh, where $h = x - l$. Hence:

$$\frac{1}{2}k(x-l)^2 = \frac{1}{2}mv^2 + mg(x-l)$$

$$v^2 = \frac{k}{m}(x-l)^2 - 2g(x-l)$$

$$\therefore v = \sqrt{\frac{k}{m}(x-l)^2 - 2g(x-l)}$$

When thrown vertically, at its maximum height all kinetic energy will have converted to gravitational potential energy. Hence:

$$\frac{1}{2}mv^2 = mgh$$

$$h = \frac{v^2}{2g} = \frac{k}{2gm}(x-l)^2 - 2g(x-l)$$

Question 23

To fly undeflected, there must be no resultant force on the electron, and so

$$eE = evB$$

$$v = \frac{E}{B} = \frac{1000}{10^{-5}} = 10^8 \text{ ms}^{-1}$$

The kinetic energy of the electron when it leaves the vacuum is provided by the potential energy of the accelerating voltage, which is equal to eV:

$$\frac{1}{2}mv^2 = eV$$

$$V = \frac{mv^2}{2e} = \frac{10^{-30} \times (10^8)^2}{2 \times 1.6 \times 10^{-19}} = \frac{10^{-11} \times 10^{16}}{3.2} = \frac{10^5}{3.2} = \mathbf{3.1 \times 10^4 \text{ V}}$$

Question 24

Alpha radiation only travels about 1 cm in air, so in the cases where the detector is 10 cm from the source, no alpha particles will be detected.

A sheet of aluminium will stop beta radiation, but not gamma radiation. Hence the fall in radiation of 50 counts/sec must be due to beta radiation.

When the source is removed, the only radiation is due to background radiation, which must therefore have a level of 10 counts/sec. Gamma radiation therefore accounts for $100 - 50 - 10 = 40$ counts/sec.

Finally, when the source is placed 1 cm from the detector, all forms of radiation (including alpha) will be observed. Hence alpha radiation is $400 - 50 - 10 - 40 = 300$ counts/sec. Therefore,

$$\text{alpha: beta: gamma} = 300:50:40 = \mathbf{30:5:4}$$

Question 25

Note that there is a mistake in this question: statement C should state "The base area (i.e. width times length) of a large box is 9 times **larger** than the base area of the small box."

Let $x = \frac{height}{width}$ and $y = \frac{length}{width}$, then the dimensions of the boxes can be written as follows:

	Width	Height	Length
Small	s	sx	sy
Medium	m	mx	my
Large	l	lx	ly

Using these expressions in statements A-E gives

A: $8s(sx)(sy) = m(mx)(my)$

$8s^3 xy = m^3 xy$

$m = 2s$ \hfill (1)

B: $sy = mx$ \hfill (2)

C: $l(ly) = 9s(sy)$

$l^2 y = 9s^2 y$

$l = 3s$ \hfill (3)

D: $sy + my + ly = 2.4$

$y(s + m + l) = 2.4$ \hfill (4)

E: $m = 2sx$ \hfill (5)

Comparing (1) and (5) gives $x = 1$. Substituting this into (2) gives

~ 125 ~

$$m = sy \quad (6)$$

Comparing (1) and (6) gives $y = 2$. Substituting this, (1) and (3) into (4) gives

$$2(s + 2s + 3s) = 2.4$$

$$6s = 1.2$$

$$s = 0.2 \text{ m}$$

Substituting this back into (1) and (3) gives $m = 0.4$ m and $l = 0.6$ m.

Therefore, the lengths of each box are **0.4 m, 0.8 m** and **1.2 m**. The ratios between width, height and length are

width: height $= 1: x = 1: 1,$ **width: length** $= 1: y = 1: 2$

Question 26

All elastic potential energy in the bowstring must be transferred to kinetic energy of the arrow.

Note that the question doesn't specify whether the bowstring obeys Hooke's law or whether the bow is extended with a constant force. The assumption made here is that the bowstring does obey Hooke's law and so elastic potential energy is given by $\frac{1}{2}Fx$, but making the assumption of constant force would mean that the elastic potential energy is equal to work done in drawing back the bow, which is Fx.

$$\frac{1}{2}Fx = \frac{1}{2}mv^2$$

$$v = \sqrt{\frac{Fx}{m}} = \sqrt{\frac{120 \times 0.6}{0.02}} = \sqrt{\frac{1.2 \times 6 \times 10^2 \times 10^{-1}}{2 \times 10^{-2}}}$$

$$v = \sqrt{3.6 \times 10^3} = \sqrt{36 \times 10^2} = \mathbf{60 \text{ ms}^{-1}}$$

(assuming constant force would give a speed of $60\sqrt{2}$ ms^{-1})

The actual kinetic energy obtained by the arrow is

$$h \times \frac{1}{2}Fx = \frac{25}{36} \times \frac{1}{2} \times 120 \times 0.6 = \frac{25}{36} \times 36 = 25 \text{ J}$$

$$\frac{1}{2}mv^2 = 25$$

$$v = \sqrt{\frac{25 \times 2}{0.02}} = \sqrt{2500} = \mathbf{50 \text{ ms}^{-1}}$$

Since there is no horizontal acceleration, the arrow travels at a constant speed:

$$t = \frac{d}{v} = \frac{50}{50} = 1 \text{ s}$$

Consider the vertical displacement during the 1 second:

$$s = ut + \frac{1}{2}at^2 = \frac{1}{2} \times 10 \times 1^2 = 5 \text{ m}$$

Hence the arrow must be aimed **5 m** above the centre of the target.

The horizontal speed of the arrow is $v_x = 50 \text{ ms}^{-1}$, and the vertical speed is

$$v_y = u + at = 10 \times 1 = 10 \text{ ms}^{-1}$$

Hence the arrow's overall speed, V, is given by

$$V^2 = v_x^2 + v_y^2 = 50^2 + 10^2 = 2600 \text{ (ms}^{-1})^2$$

The kinetic energy of the arrow just before striking the target is therefore

$$KE_{total} = \frac{1}{2}mV^2 = \frac{1}{2} \times 0.02 \times 2600 = 26 \text{ J}$$

Work done to bring the arrow to a stop is given by $W = Fx$ and so

$$F \times 5 \times 10^{-3} = 26$$

$$F = 5.2 \times 10^3 = \textbf{5200 N}$$

Consider conservation of momentum, where the initial momentum of the target is zero:

$$m_{arrow} \times v_{arrow} = (m_{arrow} + m_{target}) \times v_{target}$$

$$0.02 \times \sqrt{2600} = (0.02 + 5) \times v_{target}$$

$$v_{target} = \frac{0.02 \times 10\sqrt{26}}{5.02}$$

$$v_{target} \approx \frac{0.02 \times 10 \times 5}{5} = \mathbf{0.2 \ ms^{-1}}$$

END OF PAPER

2012

PART A

Question 1

A sketch of the function is as follows:

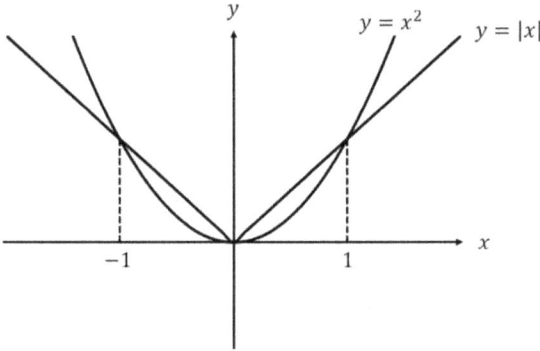

The area included can be calculated by integration, noting that the area is symmetrical about the y-axis:

$$A = 2\int_0^1 (x - x^2)\, dx = 2\left[\frac{x^2}{2} - \frac{x^3}{3}\right]_0^1 = 2\left(\frac{1}{2} - \frac{1}{3}\right) = \frac{1}{3}$$

Question 2

i) Use the standard formula for a binomial expansion:

$$(4+x)^4 = 4^4 + 4(4)^3 x + 6(4)^2 x^2 + 4(4)x^3 + x^4$$

$$= 256 + 256x + 96x^2 + 16x^3 + x^4$$

ii) In this case, $x = 0.2$. Substituting into the above equation gives

$$(4.2)^4 = 256 + 256(0.2) + 96(0.2)^2 + 16(0.2)^3 + (0.2)^4$$

$$= 256 + 51.2 + 3.84 + 0.128 + 0.0016 = \mathbf{311.17}$$

Question 3

Separate the summation into two and use the formula for the sum of a geometric series on the second part:

$$\sum_{r=1}^{8}(2+4^r) = \sum_{r=1}^{8} 2 + \sum_{r=1}^{8} 4^r = (8 \times 2) + (4 + 4^2 + 4^3 + \cdots + 4^8)$$

$$= 16 + \frac{4(4^8-1)}{4-1} = 16 + \frac{4(65535)}{3} = 16 + 4 \times 21845 = \mathbf{87396}$$

Question 4

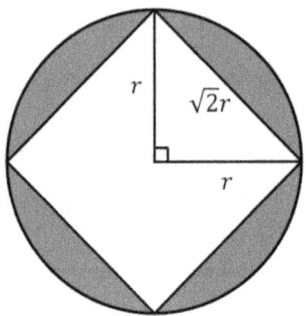

As shown in the diagram, the side length of the square is $\sqrt{2}r$. Hence, the area of the shaded region is

$$A = A_{circle} - A_{square}$$

$$A = \pi r^2 - \left(\sqrt{2}r\right)^2 = \left(\pi - 2\right)r^2$$

Question 5

Let $f(x) = x^3 - 6x^2 - 9x + 14$.

$$f(1) = 1^3 - 6(1)^2 - 9(1) + 14 = 1 - 6 - 9 + 14 = 0$$

Therefore $x = 1$ is a solution to $f(x) = 0$. This also means that $(x - 1)$ is a factor of $f(x)$:

$$x^3 - 6x^2 - 9x + 14 = (x - 1)(x^2 - 5x - 14) = 0$$

$$(x - 1)(x - 7)(x + 2) = 0$$

$$\therefore x = 1, 7, -2$$

Question 6

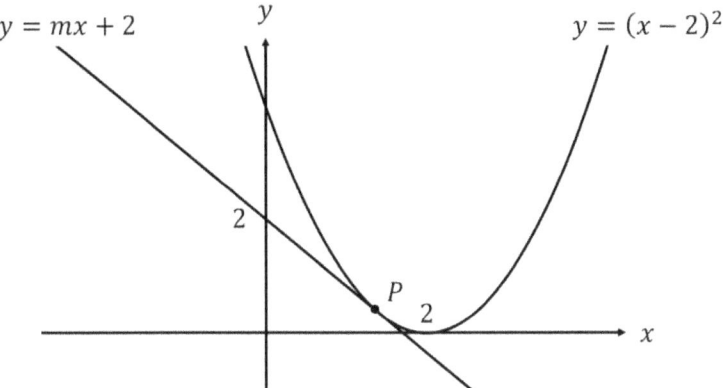

At P,

$$y = mx + 2 = (x-2)^2$$

$$mx + 2 = x^2 - 4x + 4$$

$$0 = x^2 - (4+m)x + 2 \quad (1)$$

Also, the gradient of the curve at P must be equal to m:

$$\frac{dy}{dy} = 2(x-2) = m$$

$$m = 2x - 4$$

Substitute this expression for m into (1):

$$0 = x^2 - (4 + 2x - 4)x + 2$$

$$0 = x^2 - 2x^2 + 2$$

$$x^2 - 2 = 0$$

$$x = \pm\sqrt{2}$$

As the question states that $x > 0$, $x = \sqrt{2}$.

$$m = 2\sqrt{2} - 4$$

$$y = (2\sqrt{2} - 4)x + 2$$

Question 7

$\log_2 16 = 4$ and $\log_{10} \sqrt{0.01} = \log_{10} 0.1 = -1$. Hence,

$$5 = \log_2 16 + \log_{10} \sqrt{0.01} + \log_3 x$$

$$5 = 4 - 1 + \log_3 x$$

$$\log_3 x = 2$$

$$x = 9$$

Question 8

To obtain a total score of 7, the following combinations are possible: $(6, 1)$, $(5, 2)$ and $(4, 3)$.

$$P(6, 1) = \frac{1}{6} \times \frac{1}{3} = \frac{1}{18}$$

$$P(5, 2) = \frac{1}{6} \times \frac{1}{3} = \frac{1}{18}$$

$$P(4, 2) = \frac{1}{6} \times \frac{1}{3} = \frac{1}{18}$$

The total probability is therefore

$$3 \times \frac{1}{18} = \frac{1}{6}$$

Question 9

Use the identity $\sin^2 \theta + \cos^2 \theta = 1$:

$$\cos^2 \theta + \sin \theta = 0$$

$$(1 - \sin^2 \theta) + \sin \theta = 0$$

$$\sin^2 \theta - \sin \theta - 1 = 0$$

This is a quadratic function in $\sin \theta$, hence it can be solved using the quadratic formula:

$$\sin \theta = \frac{1 \pm \sqrt{1 - 4(1)(-1)}}{2} = \frac{1 \pm \sqrt{5}}{2}$$

Since $-1 \leq \sin \theta \leq 1$,

$$\sin \theta = \frac{1 - \sqrt{5}}{2}$$

Question 10

From (c), the curve must have a single stationary point at $x = 4$. This cannot be a point of inflection due to (d), and so must be a maximum or a minimum. From (d), there are points of inflection (but not stationary points) at both $x = 2$ and $x = 6$. An example of the function is therefore shown below:

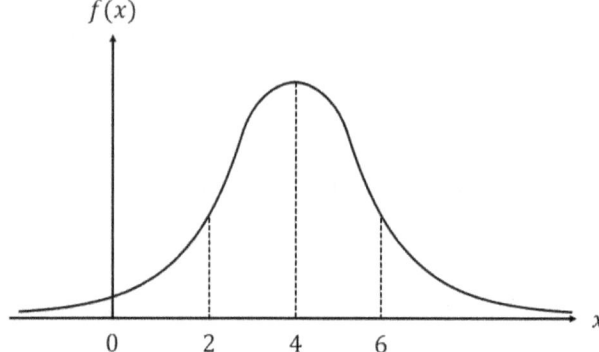

Note also that the function must always be above the x-axis due to (a) and continuous due to (b).

Question 11

We can split this inequality into two:

$$-1 < -\frac{1}{x} + 2x \quad (1)$$

$$-\frac{1}{x} + 2x < 1 \quad (2)$$

(1)

$$-1 < -\frac{1}{x} + 2x$$

$$-x^2 < -x + 2x^3$$

$$0 < 2x^3 + x^2 - x$$

$$0 < x(2x-1)(x+1)$$

```
   −     +      −      +
  −1     0    1/2
───o─────o─────o─────────→ x
```

(2)

$$-\frac{1}{x} + 2x < 1$$

$$-x + 2x^3 < x^2$$

$$2x^3 - x^2 - x < 0$$

$$x(2x+1)(x-1) < 0$$

```
   −     +      −      +
       −1/2    0       1
───────o─────o─────o─────→ x
```

Combining the two number lines, both inequalities are satisfied when

$$-1 < x < -\frac{1}{2} \text{ and } \frac{1}{2} < x < 1$$

$$\frac{1}{2} < |x| < 1$$

Question 12

First, consider what happens at large values of x and when $x \to 0$:

When $x \to +\infty$, $y \to \dfrac{-x^2}{x^2} = -1$.

When $x \to -\infty$, $y \to \dfrac{-x^2}{x^2} = -1$.

When $x \to 0$, $y \to \infty$.

Also, find the points of intersection of the graph with the x-axis:

When $y = 0$,
$$1 - x - x^2 = 0$$
$$x^2 + x - 1 = 0$$
$$x = \frac{-1 \pm \sqrt{1 - 4(1)(-1)}}{2} = \frac{-1 \pm \sqrt{5}}{2}$$

Finally, find any stationary points on the graph:
$$y = x^{-2} - x^{-1} - 1$$
$$\frac{dy}{dx} = -2x^{-3} + x^{-2} = 0$$
$$-2 + x = 0$$
$$x = 2$$

At $x = 2$, $y = \dfrac{1 - 2 - 2^2}{2^2} = -\dfrac{5}{4}$.

Hence the sketch is shown below:

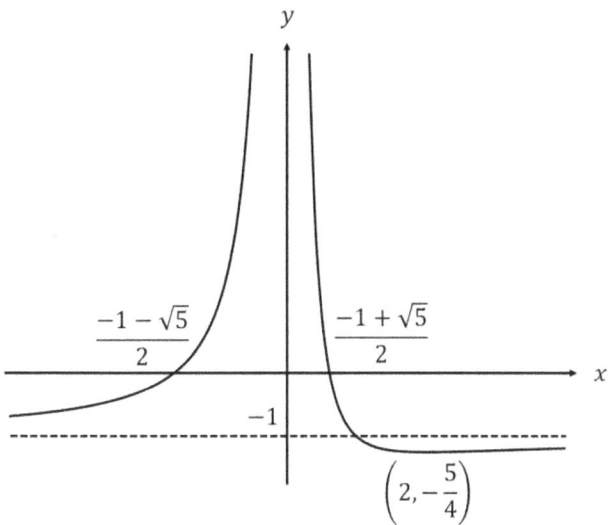

END OF SECTION

PAT PAST PAPER SOLUTIONS 2013

PART B

Question 13: C

Since both the locomotive and the model are made of iron, they will have the same density. Hence, mass $\propto$ length^3:

$$\frac{6.5 \times 10^4}{10^3} = \frac{1}{l^3}$$

$$l^3 = \frac{1}{65}$$

$$l = \frac{1}{\sqrt[3]{65}} \approx \frac{1}{4} \text{ m} = \mathbf{25 \text{ cm}}$$

Question 14: D

For an ideal gas, $PV = nRT$ and $n = \frac{m}{M}$, where m is the total mass of the gas and M is its molar mass. The molar mass of carbon dioxide is

$$M = 12 + 2 \times 16 = 44 \text{ g/mol}$$

Hence,

$$P = \frac{mRT}{MV} = \frac{(88)(8.3)(273+27)}{(44)(0.02)} = 8.3 \times 300 \times 10^2$$

$$P = 24.9 \times 10^4 \text{ Pa} = \mathbf{249 \text{ kPa}}$$

PAT PAST PAPER SOLUTIONS 2013

Question 15: B

The power delivered by the battery is equal to the driving force of the car multiplied by its speed:

$$P = IV = Fv$$

In this case, F is equal to the value of air resistance since the car is moving with a constant speed. Hence,

$$F = \frac{IV}{v} = \frac{100 \times 160}{\left(36 \times \frac{1000}{3600}\right)} = \frac{1.6 \times 10^4}{10} = 1600 \text{ N}$$

Question 16: C

All smaller cubes that are painted will be those originally on the surface of the larger cube. Since the cube is divided into 125 equal pieces, each side is divided by $\sqrt[3]{125} = 5$. The unpainted cubes will therefore only be those that are part of the $3 \times 3 \times 3$ cube inside the larger cube, where none of their faces are on the outside.

Hence there are $3 \times 3 \times 3 = $ **27** unpainted cubes.

Question 17: A

The slider goes not get to T. The slider converts potential energy to kinetic energy, and then back to potential energy as it rises again. Based on conservation of energy, the slider would be able to reach a height of T again. However, in order to remain in contact with the track, the component of the slider's weight perpendicular to the slope must be equal to the centripetal force $\left(\frac{mv^2}{r}\right)$ required to continue along the circular track. Since $v = 0$ at T (due to conservation of energy), then at some point before reaching T, the slider's speed will become too small to allow it to remain in contact with the track and so it will not reach T.

Question 18

a) The voltmeter must be in parallel with the resistor, whilst the ammeter must be in series:

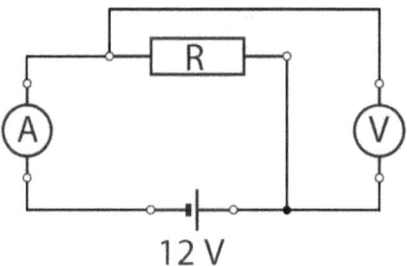

The current is $I = \dfrac{V}{R} = \dfrac{12}{2\times 10^3} = $ **6 mA**

b) When the switch is moved to e and the circuit is closed, the capacitor is being charged. The time constant is

$$\tau = RC = 2 \times 10^3 \times 4 \times 10^{-6} = 8 \text{ ms}$$

Hence, the time after which the current is not changing significantly is $T \approx 5\tau = $ **40 ms**. The graph of current against time will therefore be

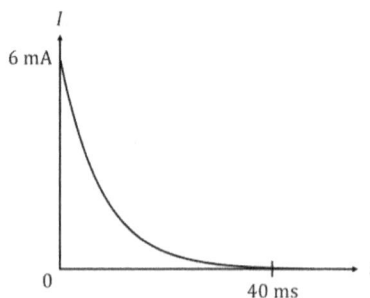

When the switch is moved to d, the capacitor is then discharging, with the same time constant. In this case, current will flow in the opposite direction. Hence, the graph of current against time will be

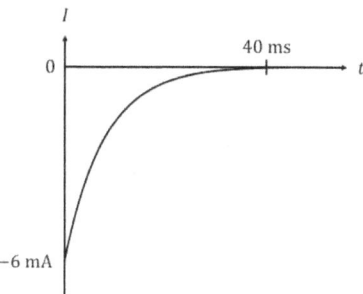

Question 19

Let the distance between the loudspeaker and the screen be d. Maximal intensity occurs when there is constructive interference, for which the path difference must be a whole number of wavelengths:

$$2d = n\lambda$$

$$d = \frac{n\lambda}{2}$$

Hence, the distance between two screen positions giving successive maxima is $\frac{\lambda}{2}$.

In order for the microphone to record minima and maxima, the distance d must change to allow for constructive or destructive interference.

In case (a) the microphone **would** record minima and maxima as d changes.

In case (b) the microphone **would not** record minima and maxima as d does not change.

Question 20

The number of nuclei of each isotope at time t is given by

$$N(t) = N(0)e^{-\lambda t}$$

where $\lambda = \frac{\ln 2}{T}$. Hence,

$$r(t) = \frac{N_{235}(t)}{N_{238}(t)} = \frac{N_{235}(0) \, e^{-\lambda_{235} t}}{N_{238}(0) \, e^{-\lambda_{238} t}}$$

Let r_0 be the initial relative abundance and since $r(10^9) = 0.0072$,

$$r_0 \frac{e^{-\lambda_{235}(10^9)}}{e^{-\lambda_{238}(10^9)}} = 0.0072$$

$$0.0072 = r_0 \frac{e^{-\frac{10^9 \times \ln 2}{T_{235}}}}{e^{-\frac{10^9 \times \ln 2}{T_{238}}}} \approx r_0 \frac{e^{-\frac{10^9 \times \left(\frac{7}{10}\right)}{7 \times 10^8}}}{e^{-\frac{10^9 \times \left(\frac{7}{10}\right)}{4.5 \times 10^9}}} = r_0 \frac{e^{-1}}{e^{-\frac{0.7}{4.5}}} = r_0 \frac{(2.7)^{-1}}{1 - \frac{0.7}{4.5}}$$

$$r_0 = \frac{0.0072 \times \left(1 - \frac{0.7}{4.5}\right)}{(2.7)^{-1}} = 0.0072 \times \frac{3.8}{4.5} \times 2.7 \approx \mathbf{0.016}$$

~ 144 ~

Question 21

For a circular orbit, the centripetal force is provided by the gravitational force:

$$\frac{GMm}{R^2} = \frac{mv^2}{R}$$

$$v = \sqrt{\frac{GM}{R}}$$

G is the gravitational constant and M is the mass of the Earth.

As the other meteoroid has the same mass and radius of orbit, from the equation above it will therefore have the same speed. Conservation of momentum therefore states that

total momentum before = total momentum after = 0

Hence, the velocity of the double mass is zero, and so the angular speed is also zero. The trajectory of the double mass will therefore be as follows:

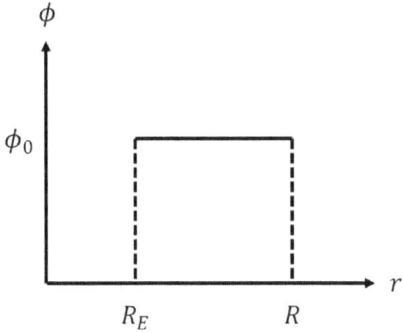

Since $GPE = -\frac{GMm}{r}$ and due to conservation of energy,

$$KE + GPE = 0$$

$$KE = \frac{GMm}{r} \propto \frac{1}{r}$$

However, when $r < 2R_E$, air resistance is significant and so reduces the kinetic energy. Also, as the mass approaches R_E, it reaches a terminal velocity.

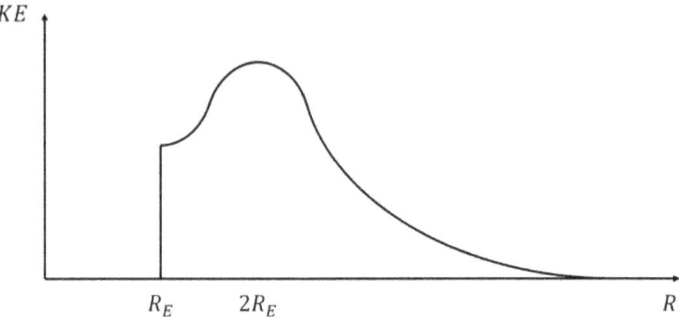

Initially, at $r = R$, temperature is very high due to the energy lost in the collision. Then, as the mass falls to Earth and r decreases, the temperature falls as the double mass cools. Once inside the Earth's atmosphere ($r \approx 2R_E$), air resistance causes energy to be dissipated as heat and so the temperature increases. When the meteorite collides with Earth ($r \approx R_E$), the loss of kinetic energy will cause the temperature to significantly increase. The graph of temperature against r is therefore

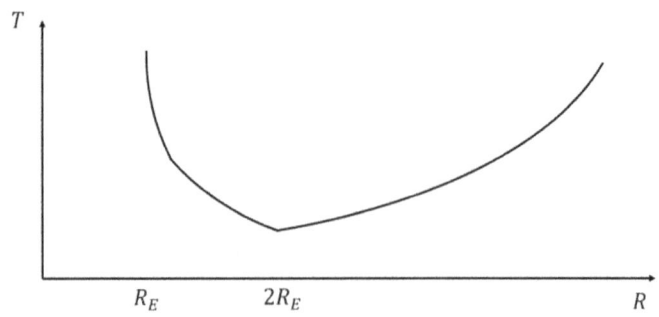

PAT PAST PAPER SOLUTIONS   2013

Question 22

a1

Throughout the motion, kinetic energy is equal to work done (as there is no friction). Since the force applied between $x = 10$ and $x = 0$ is constant at $F = -10$ N,

$$\frac{1}{2}mv^2 = \int F dx = -10(0 - 10) = 100$$

$$v = \sqrt{\frac{2 \times 100}{1}} = \sqrt{200} = 10\sqrt{2} \text{ ms}^{-1}$$

a2

$$KE = \int F dx$$

For $x > 0$, $F = -10$:

$$KE = \int F dx = -10x + c = -10x + 100$$

For $x < 0$, $F = -x - 10$:

$$KE = \int F dx = -\frac{x^2}{2} - 10x + c = -\frac{x^2}{2} - 10x + 100$$

Maximum KE occurs when $F = 0$ (at $x = -10$), so $KE_{max} = 150$ J. Kinetic energy is zero when

$$-\frac{x^2}{2} - 10x + 100 = 0$$

$$x^2 + 20x - 200 = 0$$

$$x = \frac{-20 \pm \sqrt{400 - 4(-200)}}{2} = \frac{-20 \pm \sqrt{1200}}{2} = -10 \pm 10\sqrt{3}$$

The value of x (when $x < 0$) where $KE = 0$ is therefore

$$x = -10(1 + \sqrt{3})$$

Therefore, the kinetic energy as a function of x is shown below:

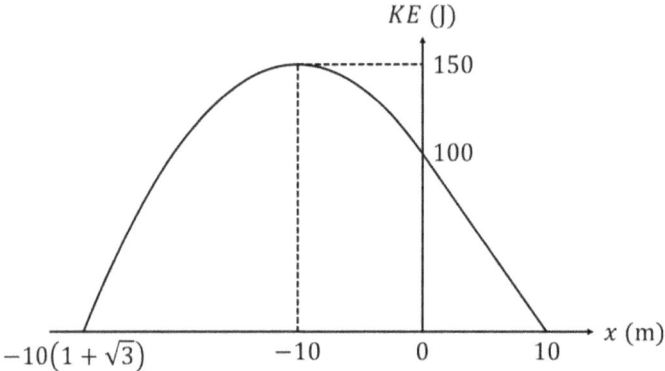

a3

Since $F = ma$ and $m = 1$ kg,

$$\frac{d^2x}{dt^2} = F$$

For $x > 0$,

$$\frac{d^2x}{dt^2} = -10$$

$$\frac{dx}{dt} = -10t + a$$

Since $\frac{dx}{dt} = 0$ when $t = 0$, $a = 0$:

$$\frac{dx}{dt} = -10t$$

The time taken to reach $x = 0$ is given by

$$s = \frac{1}{2}at^2$$

$$t = \sqrt{\frac{2s}{a}} = \sqrt{\frac{2 \times 10}{10}} = \sqrt{2} \text{ s}$$

For $x < 0$,

$$\frac{d^2x}{dt^2} = -(x + 10)$$

This is therefore simple harmonic motion, with general solution

$$x = A\sin(\omega t + \phi)$$

Since $\frac{d^2x}{dt^2} = -\omega^2 x$, $\omega = 1$. Also, the maximum acceleration occurs when speed is zero where $x = -10(1 + \sqrt{3})$:

$$A = 10(1 + \sqrt{3}) - 10 = 10\sqrt{3}$$

Therefore,

$$x = 10\sqrt{3}\sin(t + \phi)$$

The period of the motion is

$$T = \frac{2\pi}{\omega} = 2\pi$$

Therefore, during the simple harmonic motion when $x < 0$,

$$\frac{dx}{dt} = 10\sqrt{3}\cos(t + \phi)$$

$$\frac{d^2x}{dt^2} = -10\sqrt{3}\sin(t + \phi)$$

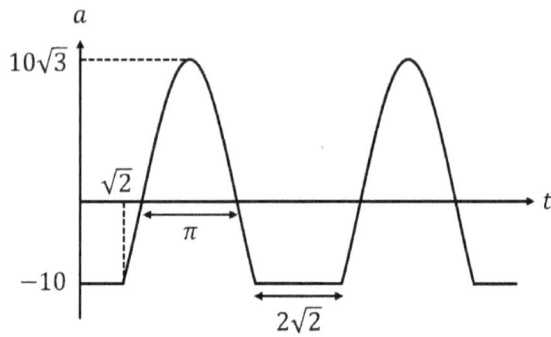

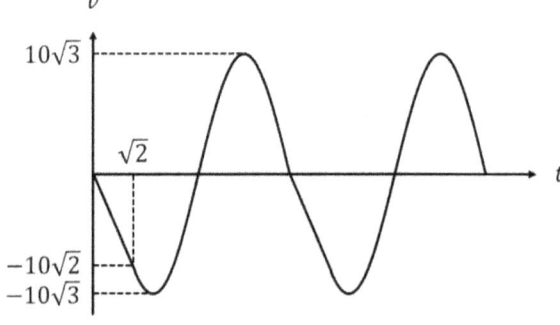

PAT PAST PAPER SOLUTIONS — 2013

b I

Consider kinetic energy:

When $x < 0$, the object loses no energy and returns at the same speed as it was when x became negative.

When $x \geq 0$, the work done against friction is equal to 1 J per metre travelled. Hence, let the initial displacement of the object be x_0. Since the object will experience a constant force of $-10 + 1 = -9$ N, its speed at $x = 0$ is

$$v^2 - u^2 = 2as$$
$$v^2 = 2 \times 9 \times x_0 = 18x_0$$

Since no energy is lost while $x < 0$, when the object again returns to the point $x = 0$, its speed will be given by $v^2 = 18x_0$. The object will now have a constant force of -11 N acting on it until it comes to rest. The distance travelled by the object before coming to rest will therefore be

$$v^2 - u^2 = 2as$$
$$0 - 18x_0 = 2 \times -11 \times s$$
$$s = \frac{18x_0}{22} = \frac{9x_0}{11}$$

This therefore applies to each successive cycle, with the mass coming to rest at a displacement of $\frac{9}{11}$ of the previous starting displacement. Eventually, as $t \to \infty$, the object will only oscillate between $x = -20$ and $x = 0$ (simple harmonic motion centred on the point $x = -10$). Hence the graph of velocity against x will be

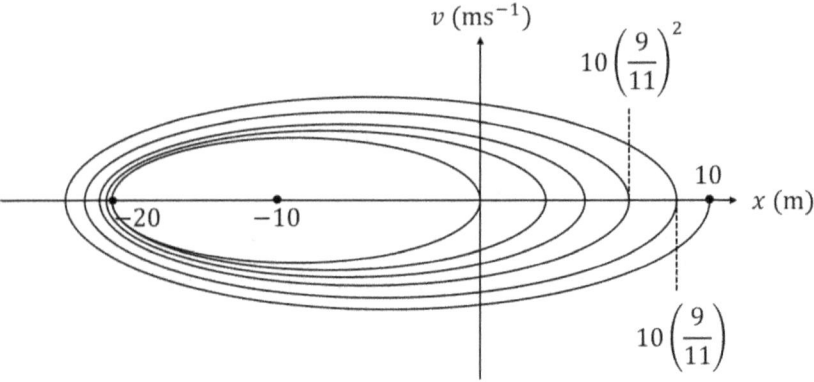

b2

The object has lost all of the initial kinetic energy that it gained from the force in $x \geq 0$, which was 100 J. Since the frictional force is always constant at 1 N, the total distance travelled when $x \geq 0$ must be

$$W = F \times d$$

$$d = \frac{100}{1} = \mathbf{100 \ m}$$

END OF PAPER

2013

PART A

Question 1

These terms form a geometric series with common ratio $r = -\frac{1}{3}$ and first term $a = \frac{2}{3}$:

$$S_\infty = \frac{a}{1-r} = \frac{\frac{2}{3}}{1-\left(-\frac{1}{3}\right)} = \frac{1}{2}$$

Question 2

Substitute y into u:

$$u = \left(\sqrt{xv} - \sqrt{x}\right)^2 = xv - 2x\sqrt{v} + x$$

$$u = x\left(v - 2\sqrt{v} + 1\right) = x\left(\sqrt{v} - 1\right)^2$$

$$x = \frac{u}{\left(\sqrt{v} - 1\right)^2}$$

Question 3

a) $P(\text{female} \cap \text{red hair}) = P(\text{female}) \times P(\text{red hair})$

$$= \frac{30}{50} \times \frac{8}{50} = \frac{3}{5} \times \frac{4}{25} = \frac{12}{125}$$

b) $P(\text{male} \cap \text{not red or black hair})$

$$= P(\text{male}) \times \left(1 - P(\text{red or black hair})\right)$$

$$= \frac{20}{50} \times \left(1 - \frac{11}{50}\right) = \frac{2}{5} \times \frac{39}{50} = \frac{39}{125}$$

Question 4

a) Substitute $x = 1$ into $f(x)$:

$$f(1) = 1^3 - 1^2 - 4(1) + 4 = 0$$

Hence, $x = 1$ is a root. This also means that $(x - 1)$ is a factor:

$$f(x) = x^3 - x^2 - 4x + 4 = (x - 1)(x^2 - 4)$$

$$f(x) = (x - 1)(x + 2)(x - 2)$$

The other two roots are therefore $x = -2$ and $x = 2$.

b) The two smallest roots are $x = -2$ and $x = 1$. The area is therefore found by integration:

$$A = \int_{-2}^{1} (x^3 - x^2 - 4x + 4)\, dx = \left[\frac{x^4}{4} - \frac{x^3}{3} - 2x^2 + 4x\right]_{-2}^{1}$$

$$A = \left(\frac{1}{4} - \frac{1}{3} - 2 + 4\right) - \left(\frac{16}{4} - \frac{-8}{3} - 2 \times 4 - 8\right)$$

$$A = \frac{1}{4} - \frac{1}{3} + 2 - 4 - \frac{8}{3} + 16 = \frac{1}{4} + 14 - \frac{9}{3} = 11 + \frac{1}{4} = \frac{45}{4}$$

Question 5

Equate both expressions for x:

$$\log_{10} 100 + \log_5 \sqrt{25} - \log_3 y^2 = 2(\log_2 8 - 9\log_{10} \sqrt{10} + 2\log_3 y)$$

$$2 + 1 - 2\log_3 y = 2\left(3 - 9\left(\frac{1}{2}\right) + 2\log_3 y\right)$$

$$3 - 2\log_3 y = -3 + 4\log_3 y$$

$$6 = 6\log_3 y$$

$$\log_3 y = 1$$

$$y = 3$$

$$x = \log_{10} 100 + \log_5 \sqrt{25} - \log_3 y^2 = 2 + 1 - \log_3(3)^2 = 2 + 1 - 2$$

$$x = 1$$

Question 6

Consider the first circle:

$$x^2 + 4x + y^2 - 2y = -1$$
$$(x+2)^2 - 4 + (y-1)^2 - 1 = -1$$
$$(x+2)^2 + (y-1)^2 = 4$$

The centre of this circle is therefore $(-2, 1)$. Now consider the second circle:

$$x^2 - 4x + y^2 - 6y = 3$$
$$(x-2)^2 - 4 + (y-3)^2 - 9 = 3$$
$$(x-2)^2 + (y-3)^2 = 16$$

The centre of the second circle is therefore $(2, 3)$. The gradient of the line passing through these points is

$$m = \frac{y_2 - y_1}{x_2 - x_1} = \frac{3-1}{2-(-2)} = \frac{2}{4} = \frac{1}{2}$$

Hence, the equation of the line is

$$y - y_1 = m(x - x_1)$$
$$y - 3 = \frac{1}{2}(x - 2)$$
$$y = \frac{1}{2}x + 2$$

Question 7

$$(3.12)^5 = (3 + 0.12)^5$$

Consider each term in the resulting expansion:

1. 3^5
2. $5 \times 3^4 \times 0.12$
3. $10 \times 3^3 \times 0.12^2$
4. $10 \times 3^2 \times 0.12^3 = 9 \times 10 \times 1.2^3 \times 10^{-3} \approx 15 \times 10^{-2} = 0.15$
5. $5 \times 3 \times 0.12^4 = 15 \times 1.2^4 \times 10^{-4} \approx 30 \times 10^{-4} = 0.003 < 0.01$

Therefore, only the first **four** terms are required.

Question 8

When $x > 0$,

$$y > \frac{1}{x}, y < \frac{2}{x}, y > \frac{x}{2}, y < 2x$$

When $x < 0$,

$$y < \frac{1}{x}, y > \frac{2}{x}, y < \frac{x}{2}, y > 2x$$

Hence, the graph is as follows:

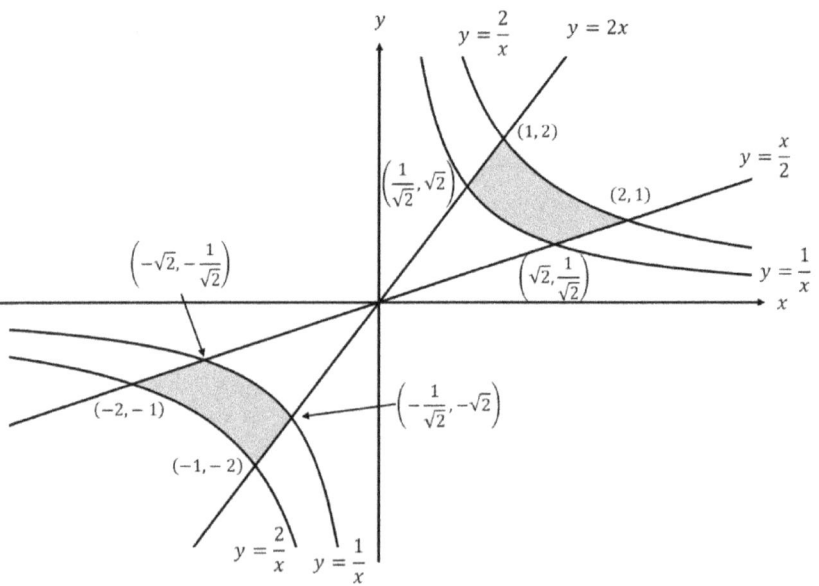

PAT PAST PAPER SOLUTIONS 2013

Question 9

a)

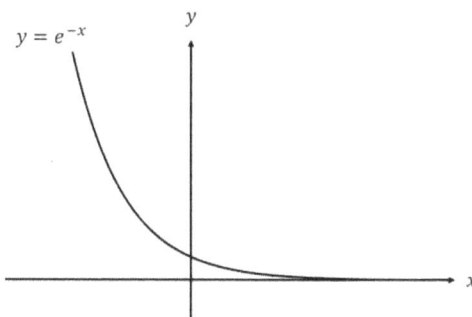

b) $y = 3\{\exp[-2(x-1)] - 2\exp[-(x-1)]\}$

First, consider what happens when $x \to \infty$ and when $x = 0$:

When $x \to \infty$, $y \to 0$ and $y < 0$.

When $x = 0$, $y = 3(e^2 - 2e)$.

Now consider any points where the graph crosses the y-axis:

$$3\{\exp[-2(x-1)] - 2\exp[-(x-1)]\} = 0$$

$$\exp[-2(x-1)] = 2\exp[-(x-1)]$$

$$\exp[-2(x-1) + (x-1)] = 2$$

$$-2x + 2 + x - 1 = \ln 2$$

$$-x + 1 = \ln 2$$

$$x = 1 - \ln 2$$

Finally, find the coordinates of any turning points through differentiation:

$$\frac{dy}{dx} = 3\{-2\exp[-2(x-1)] + 2\exp[-(x-1)]\} = 0$$

$$\exp[-2(x-1)] = \exp[-(x-1)]$$

$$-2(x-1) = -(x-1)$$

$$-2x + 2 = -x + 1$$

$$x = 1$$

At $x = 1$, $y = 3(1 - 2) = -3$

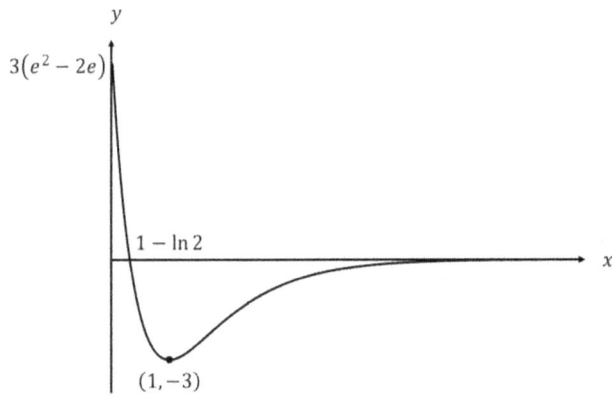

Question 10

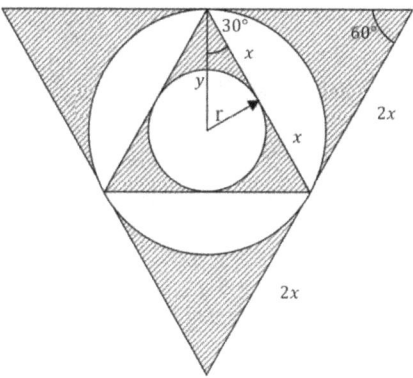

Consider the right-angled triangle inside the smaller triangle:

$$\frac{r}{x} = \tan 30 = \frac{1}{\sqrt{3}} \rightarrow x = \sqrt{3}r$$

$$\frac{r}{y} = \sin 30 = \frac{1}{2} \rightarrow y = 2r$$

Area of small circle $= \pi r^2$

Area of big circle $= \pi(2r)^2 = 4\pi r^2$

Area of small triangle $= \frac{1}{2}(2x)^2 \sin 60 = \frac{1}{2}(2\sqrt{3}r)^2 \left(\frac{\sqrt{3}}{2}\right) = 3\sqrt{3}r^2$

Area of big triangle $= \frac{1}{2}(4x)^2 \sin(60) = \frac{1}{2}(4\sqrt{3}r)^2 \left(\frac{\sqrt{3}}{2}\right) = 12\sqrt{3}r^2$

Therefore, the shaded area is

$$12\sqrt{3}r^2 - 4\pi r^2 + 3\sqrt{3}r^2 - \pi r^2 = (15\sqrt{3} - 5\pi)r^2 = \mathbf{5r^2(3\sqrt{3} - \pi)}$$

END OF SECTION

PART B

Question 11: B

As the transformer is ideal, Power in is equal to power out:

$$I_p V_p = I_s V_s$$

$$V_s = \frac{I_p V_p}{I_s} = \frac{2.4 \times 100}{4.8} = 50 \text{ V}$$

Now use the equation for the ratio of number of turns in an ideal transformer:

$$\frac{N_p}{N_s} = \frac{V_p}{V_s}$$

$$N_s = \frac{V_s}{V_p} N_p = \frac{50}{100} \times 100 = \mathbf{50 \text{ turns}}$$

Question 12: C

The number of atoms of A will halve every 3 days, whilst the number of atoms of B will halve every 6 days. Therefore,

$$A = A_0 2^{-\frac{t}{3}} \text{ and } B = B_0 2^{-\frac{t}{6}}$$

Since there are initially twice as many atoms of A as B, $A_0 = 2B_0$. To find the time at which the number of atoms of B is twice the number of atoms as A,

$$B = 2A$$

$$2\left(2B_0 2^{-\frac{t}{3}}\right) = B_0 2^{-\frac{t}{6}}$$

$$2^2 \times 2^{-\frac{t}{3}} = 2^{-\frac{t}{6}}$$

$$2^{\left(2-\frac{t}{3}\right)} = 2^{-\frac{t}{6}}$$

$$2 - \frac{t}{3} = -\frac{t}{6}$$

$$12 - 2t = -t$$

$$t = 12 \text{ days}$$

Question 13: A

When two resistors are in parallel, their total resistance is

$$R_T = \frac{R_1 R_2}{R_1 + R_2}$$

Hence, the effective resistance of the top branch of the network is

$$R_{top} = \frac{R^2}{2R} = \frac{R}{2}$$

For the bottom branch:

$$R_{bottom} = \frac{(2R)R}{2R + R} = \frac{2R^2}{3R} = \frac{2R}{3}$$

Hence, the overall resistance between A and B is

$$R_T = \frac{\left(\frac{R}{2}\right)\left(\frac{2R}{3}\right)}{\frac{R}{2} + \frac{2R}{3}} = \frac{R^2}{3} \bigg/ \frac{7R}{6} = \frac{R}{3} \times \frac{6}{7} = \frac{2R}{7}$$

Question 14: B

From Kepler's Third Law, $T^2 \propto r^3$:

$$\frac{T_1^2}{r_1^3} = \frac{T_2^2}{r_2^3}$$

$$T_2^2 = T_1^2 \left(\frac{r_2}{r_1}\right)^3 = 24^2 \times \left(\frac{1}{2}\right)^3 = \frac{24^2}{8} = 72$$

$$T_2 = \sqrt{72} \approx 8.5 \text{ hours}$$

PAT PAST PAPER SOLUTIONS — 2013

Question 15: C

Power is inversely proportional to distance squared:

$$P \propto \frac{1}{r^2}$$

$$P_1 r_1^2 = P_2 r_2^2$$

$$r_2^2 = \frac{P_1 r_1^2}{P_2} = \frac{20 \times 100^2}{10^{-3}} = 2 \times 10^8$$

$$r_2 = \sqrt{2 \times 10^8} = 10{,}000\sqrt{2} \text{ m} = \mathbf{10\sqrt{2} \text{ km}}$$

Question 16

The force through each tyre will be one quarter of the weight of the car, and force and pressure are then related by

$$p = \frac{F}{A}$$

$$A = \frac{F}{p} = \frac{\left(\frac{mg}{4}\right)}{2 \times 10^5} = \frac{10^4}{8 \times 10^5} = \frac{1}{80} = \mathbf{0.0125 \text{ m}^2}$$

Question 17

We can sketch the forces acting on the masses as follows:

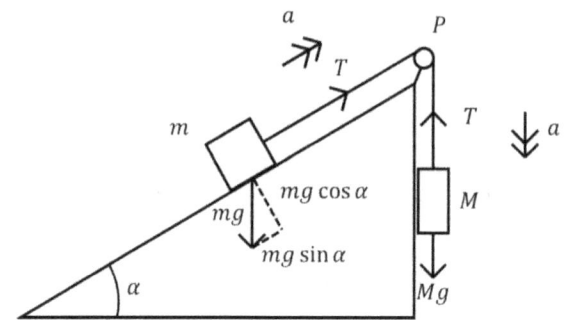

For M:

$$Mg - T = Ma$$

$$T = Mg - Ma \quad (1)$$

For m:

$$T - mg \sin \alpha = ma$$

$$T = ma + mg \sin \alpha \quad (2)$$

Set (1) equal to (2):

$$Mg - Ma = ma + mg \sin \alpha$$

$$a(M + m) = Mg - mg \sin \alpha$$

$$a = \frac{g(M - m \sin \alpha)}{M + m}$$

Substitute this back into (1):

$$T = Mg - \frac{Mg(M - m \sin \alpha)}{M + m}$$

$$T = Mg\left(\frac{M + m - (M - m\sin\alpha)}{M + m}\right)$$

$$T = \frac{mgM(1 + \sin\alpha)}{M + m}$$

For the masses to be stationary, $a = 0$. Using the previous equation for acceleration,

$$M = m\sin\alpha$$

$$\sin\alpha = \frac{M}{m}$$

Question 18

Using conservation of momentum the velocity of the combined object immediately after the collision can be calculated:

$$mv_p = (M + m)v_2$$

$$v_2 = \frac{mv_p}{M + m} = \frac{0.2 \times 122}{12.2} = 2 \text{ ms}^{-1}$$

Conservation of energy then shows that all kinetic energy of the ball must be converted to potential energy at its maximum height:

$$\frac{1}{2}(M + m)v_2^2 = (M + m)gh$$

$$h = \frac{v_2^2}{2g} = \frac{2^2}{20} = \frac{1}{5} = \mathbf{0.2 \text{ m}}$$

PAT PAST PAPER SOLUTIONS 2013

Question 19

The narrow slits act like coherent sources, as they have a constant phase difference between them. When light from the sources arrives at a particular point on the screen, it will have travelled different distances and hence there will be a path difference.

When the path difference is an integer multiple of the wavelength, light from the two sources arrives in phase and so there is constructive interference (a maximum). When the path difference is a half-integer multiple of the wavelength, light arrives out of phase and so there is destructive interference (a minimum). This results in the pattern shown below.

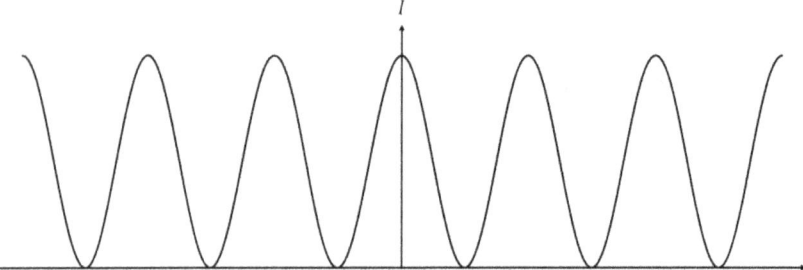

Green light has a shorter wavelength than red light and so, since fringe separation is proportional to wavelength, the maxima and minima will be closer together.

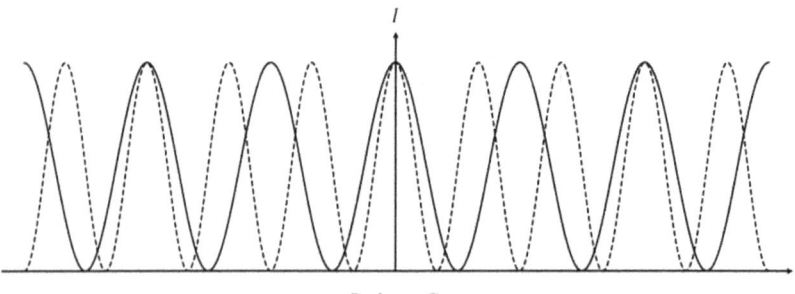

——Red ----Green

PAT PAST PAPER SOLUTIONS 2013

Question 20

The mass of water is equal to the volume multiplied by the density, which is $10 \times 10 \times 15 \times 1 = 1500$ g $= 1.5$ kg.

The energy required to heat the water to boiling point ($100°C$) is

$$E = mc\Delta T = 1.5 \times 4.2 \times (100 - 20) = 1.5 \times 4.2 \times 80$$

$$E = 120 \times 4.2 = \mathbf{504 \text{ kJ}}$$

The reduction in boiling point with altitude is due to the **decrease in atmospheric pressure.**

At 6000 m, the boiling point of water is $100 - \frac{6000}{300} = 100 - 20 = 80°C$. Therefore, the energy required to boil the water at this altitude is

$$E_{6000} = 0.1 \times 4.2 \times (80 - 10) = 0.1 \times 4.2 \times 70 = \mathbf{29.4 \text{ kJ}}$$

Boiling a full pot at sea level requires 504 kJ and takes 15 minutes. At 6000 m, boiling the water requires 29.4 kJ and the stove will take twice as long to produce each unit of energy as it operates at 50% power. Hence, the time taken is

$$\frac{29.4}{504} \times 15 \times 2 = \frac{0.1 \times 4.2 \times 70}{120 \times 4.2} \times 30 = \frac{7}{4} \text{ mins} = \mathbf{105 \text{ s}}$$

Question 21

a) The acceleration experienced by the particle is $a = \frac{f}{m}$. Hence, the velocity of the particle as it leaves the region of acceleration is

$$v^2 = u^2 + 2as = v_0^2 + 2\left(\frac{f}{m}\right)d$$

$$v = \sqrt{v_0^2 + \frac{2fd}{m}}$$

b) Since the force F is always perpendicular to the velocity of the particle, its motion will be circular, with radius R, and it will move at the same constant speed, v.

$$F = \frac{mv^2}{R} = \alpha v$$

$$R = \frac{mv}{\alpha}$$

The point where the particle hits the detector is therefore at a distance of $2R$ from the point where it enters the region. Hence the y coordinate where the particle is detected is

$$y = 2R = \frac{2mv}{\alpha}$$

where $v = \sqrt{v_0^2 + \frac{2fd}{m}}$ from part (a).

c) Consider two particles, with speeds v_a and v_b, where $v_b = v_a + \Delta v$:

$$y_a = \frac{2mv_a}{\alpha}$$

$$y_b = \frac{2mv_b}{\alpha} = \frac{2m}{\alpha}(v_a + \Delta v) = y_a + \frac{2m\Delta v}{\alpha}$$

To ensure the particles can be distinguished,

$$y_b > y_a + \Delta y$$

$$y_a + \frac{2m\Delta v}{\alpha} > y_a + \Delta y$$

$$\Delta v > \frac{\alpha \Delta y}{2m}$$

d) During the initial region of acceleration, the word done is equal to the force applied multiplied by distance:

$$W = fd$$

In the region of circular motion, the force F does no work on the particle as the force never acts in the direction of motion of the particle. Hence the total work done by both forces is fd.

END OF PAPER

2014

PART A

Question 1

Let there be x green buttons in the jar. There are therefore $2x$ yellow buttons, $4x$ red buttons and $8x$ blue buttons. Hence there are a total of $x + 2x + 4x + 8x = 15x$ buttons in the jar.

a) $P(b) = \frac{8}{15}$

b) $P(r) = \frac{4}{15}$

c) $P(y) = \frac{2}{15}$

d) $P(g) = \frac{1}{15}$

Question 2

This is geometric series with first term 1 and common ratio e^{-x}. Hence,

$$S_\infty = \frac{a}{1-r} = \frac{1}{1-e^{-x}}$$

The sum to infinity only converges if $|r| < 1$. Hence,

$$|e^{-x}| < 1$$

$$x > 0$$

Question 3

a) Since $\cos x = \frac{d}{dx}(1 + \sin x)$,

$$\int_0^{\frac{\pi}{2}} \frac{\cos x}{1 + \sin x} dx = [\ln(1 + \sin x)]_0^{\frac{\pi}{2}}$$

$$= \ln 2 - \ln 1 = \mathbf{\ln 2}$$

b) Use partial fractions to separate the integral into two:

$$\frac{x}{x^2 + 6x + 8} = \frac{x}{(x+4)(x+2)} = \frac{A}{x+4} + \frac{B}{x+2}$$

$$\frac{x}{(x+4)(x+2)} = \frac{A(x+2) + B(x+4)}{(x+4)(x+2)}$$

$$A + B = 1 \quad (1)$$

$$2A + 4B = 0$$

$$A + 2B = 0 \quad (2)$$

$(2) - (1)$ and then substitute back into (1):

$$B = -1 \text{ and } A = 2$$

Hence,

$$\int_0^2 \frac{x}{x^2 + 6x + 8} dx = \int_0^2 \left(\frac{2}{x+4} - \frac{1}{x+2} \right) dx$$

$$= [2\ln(x+4) - \ln(x+2)]_0^2$$

$$= (2\ln 6 - \ln 4) - (2\ln 4 - \ln 2) = 2\ln 6 - 3\ln 4 + \ln 2$$

$$= \ln(6^2) - \ln(4^3) + \ln 2 = \ln\left(\frac{6^2 \times 2}{4^3}\right) = \ln\left(\frac{72}{64}\right) = \mathbf{\ln\left(\frac{9}{8}\right)}$$

Question 4

The expression can initially be simplified and then expanded:

$$(1 + 2x)^4(1 - 2x)^6 = [(1 + 2x)^4(1 - 2x)^4](1 - 2x)^2$$

$$= (1 - 4x^2)^4(1 - 2x)^2$$

$$= [1 + 4(-4x^2) + 6(-4x^2)^2 + 4(-4x^2)^3 + (-4x^2)^4][1 - 4x + 4x^2]$$

The x^7 term is therefore

$$4(-4x^2)^3(-4x) = 4^5 x^7 = 1024 x^7$$

The coefficient of x^7 is therefore **1024**.

Question 5

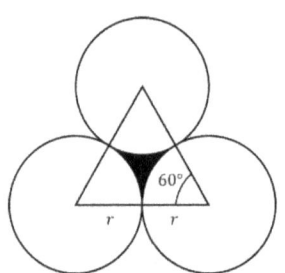

$$A = A_{triangle} - 3 A_{sector}$$

$$A_{triangle} = \frac{1}{2}(2r)^2 \sin 60 = 2r^2 \left(\frac{\sqrt{3}}{2}\right) = \sqrt{3} r^2$$

$$A_{sector} = \frac{60}{360} \times \pi r^2 = \frac{\pi r^2}{6}$$

$$\therefore A = \sqrt{3} r^2 - 3 \times \frac{\pi r^2}{6} = \left(\sqrt{3} - \frac{\pi}{2}\right) r^2$$

Question 6

The total volume of the snowman is

$$V_{snowman} = \frac{4}{3}\pi r^3 + \frac{4}{3}\pi(2r)^3 = \frac{4}{3}\pi \times 9r^3 = 12\pi r^3$$

The volume of the cylinder, in terms of its length l, is

$$V_{cylinder} = \pi \left(\frac{r}{2}\right)^2 l$$

$$V_{snowman} = V_{cylinder}$$

$$12\pi r^3 = \frac{\pi r^2 l}{4}$$

$$\boldsymbol{l = 48r}$$

Question 7

A sketch of the region is shown below:

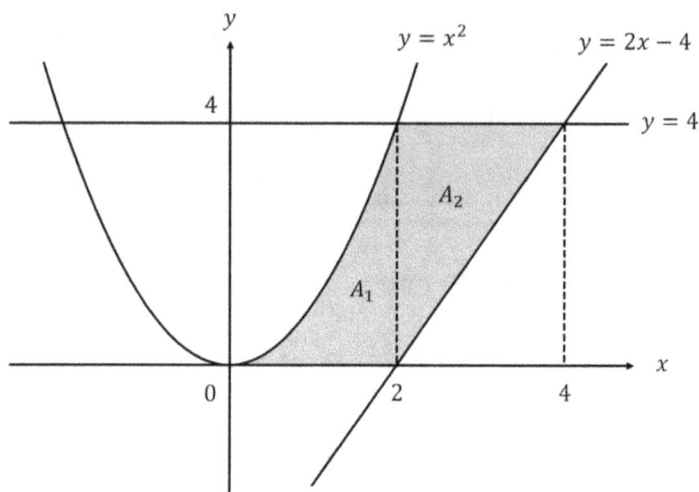

The area can be divided into A_1 and A_2 as shown on the sketch.

$$A_1 = \int_0^2 x^2 \, dx = \left[\frac{x^3}{3}\right]_0^2 = \frac{8}{3}$$

$$A_2 = \frac{1}{2} \times 2 \times 4 = 4$$

Hence, the total area is

$$4 + \frac{8}{3} = \frac{20}{3}$$

Question 8

$f(x)$ and its first, second and third derivatives for $x < 0$ and $x \geq 0$ are shown in the table below:

	$x < 0$	$x \geq 0$
$f(x)$	e^x	$e^{-x} + 2x$
$f'(x)$	e^x	$-e^{-x} + 2$
$f''(x)$	e^x	e^{-x}
$f'''(x)$	e^x	$-e^{-x}$

The sketches of $f(x)$ and its derivatives are shown below:

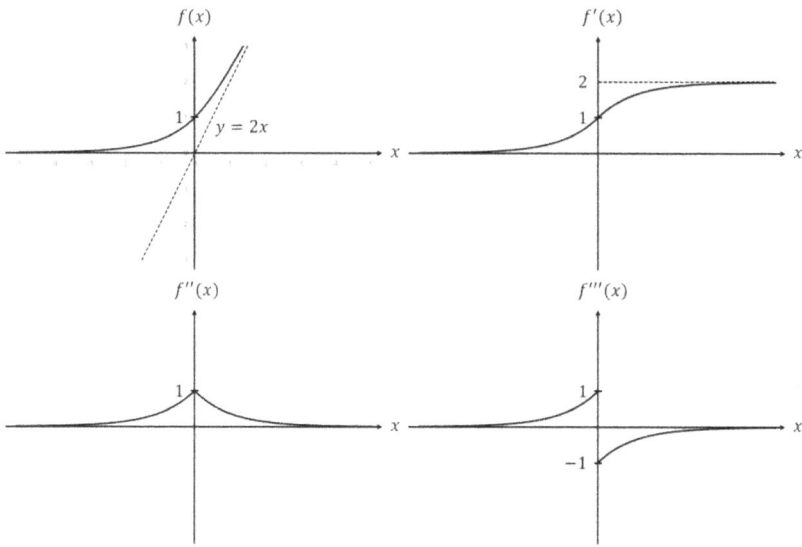

Question 9

The circle must have a radius of $\sqrt{5}$ and centre $(0, 0)$, as shown below:

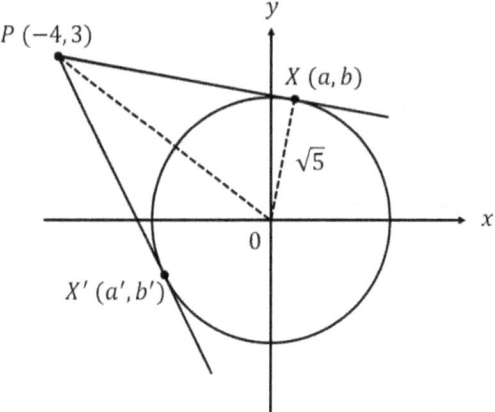

The length OP is given by $OP^2 = 3^2 + (-4)^2 = 25$. Then, using Pythagoras' theorem:

$$PX^2 = PX'^2 = OP^2 - OX^2 = 25 - 5 = 20$$

Then, consider the lengths of PX and OX to find (a, b):

$$PX^2 = 20 = \big(a - (-4)\big)^2 + (b - 3)^2$$

$$a^2 + 8a + 16 + b^2 - 6b + 9 = 20$$

$$a^2 + 8a + b^2 - 6b = -5 \quad (1)$$

$$OX^2 = 5 = a^2 + b^2 \quad (2)$$

(1) − (2):

$$8a - 6b = -10$$

$$b = \frac{4a + 5}{3} \quad (3)$$

Substitute (3) into (2):

$$a^2 + \left(\frac{4a + 5}{3}\right)^2 = 5$$

$$9a^2 + 16a^2 + 40a + 25 = 45$$

$$25a^2 + 40a - 20 = 0$$

$$5a^2 + 8a - 4 = 0$$

$$(5a - 2)(a + 2) = 0$$

Hence $a = \frac{2}{5}$ or $a = -2$. Substitute this back into (3) to get $b = \frac{11}{5}$ or $b = -1$.

Therefore, $X = \left(\frac{2}{5}, \frac{11}{5}\right)$ and $X' = (-2, -1)$. The gradients of each line can then be found:

$$m_{PX} = \frac{\frac{11}{5} - 3}{\frac{2}{5} - (-4)} = \frac{11 - 15}{2 + 20} = -\frac{2}{11}$$

$$m_{PX'} = \frac{-1 - 3}{-2 - (-4)} = -2$$

The equations of each line are therefore:

PX:

$$y - 3 = -\frac{2}{11}(x + 4)$$

$$y = -\frac{2}{11}x + \frac{25}{11}$$

PX':

$$y - 3 = -2(x + 4)$$

$$y = -2x - 5$$

END OF SECTION

PAT PAST PAPER SOLUTIONS — 2014

PART B:

Question 10: D

Statement i) is not correct as the duration of the day depends on the planet's own rotation. Statement ii) is correct because the further away a planet is from the sun, the longer the duration of its year (Kepler's 3rd Law). Statement iii) is not correct as Jupiter is the largest planet. Statement iv) is not correct as Uranus and Neptune have fewer moons than Jupiter and Saturn. Lastly, statement v) is correct as the closest four planets (Mercury to Mars) are rock, whereas the further four planets (Jupiter to Neptune) are gas giants.

Question 11: C

A wave of frequency 100 GHz has a wavelength of

$$\lambda = \frac{c}{f} = \frac{3 \times 10^8}{10^{11}} = 3 \text{ mm}$$

This is in the range of **microwaves**.

Question 12: A

Since the object's relative velocity with respect to the ISS can be neglected, it follows the ISS with the same speed. Hence, its centripetal acceleration will be equal to the gravitational acceleration from the Earth and so it will continue following the ISS in its orbit.

Question 13

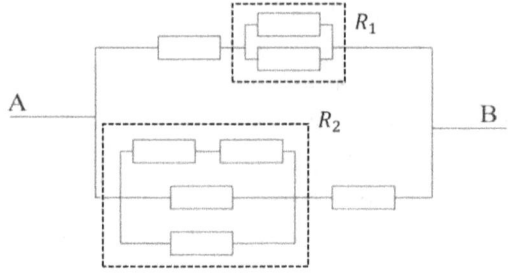

For resistors in parallel, the total resistance is given by

$$\frac{1}{R_T} = \frac{1}{R_1} + \frac{1}{R_2} + \cdots + \frac{1}{R_n}$$

Hence, the resistance of R_1 is

$$\frac{1}{R_1} = \frac{1}{R} + \frac{1}{R} = \frac{2}{R}$$

$$R_1 = \frac{R}{2}$$

The resistance of the top line is therefore $R_{top} = R + \frac{R}{2} = \frac{3R}{2}$. The resistance of R_2 is given by

$$\frac{1}{R_2} = \frac{1}{2R} + \frac{1}{R} + \frac{1}{R} = \frac{5}{2R}$$

$$R_2 = \frac{2R}{5}$$

The resistance of the bottom line is therefore $R_{bottom} = \frac{2R}{5} + R = \frac{7R}{5}$.

The total resistance between A and B is

$$\frac{1}{R_T} = \frac{1}{R_{top}} + \frac{1}{R_{bottom}} = \frac{2}{3R} + \frac{5}{7R} = \frac{29}{21R}$$

$$R_T = \frac{21R}{29}$$

Question 14

For a mass-spring system, the oscillation period is related to the mass, m, and the spring constant, k, by

$$T = 2\pi\sqrt{\frac{m}{k}}$$

When the two springs are in series, the effective spring constant is $\frac{k}{2}$, and so the period will be

$$T_{series} = 2\pi\sqrt{\frac{m}{k/2}} = 2\pi\sqrt{\frac{2m}{k}} = \sqrt{2}T$$

When the two springs are in parallel, the effective spring constant is $2k$, and so the period will be

$$T_{parallel} = 2\pi\sqrt{\frac{m}{2k}} = \frac{T}{\sqrt{2}}$$

As the period of oscillation does not depend on gravitational acceleration, on a planet with surface gravity $2g$ **the period would be the same.**

Question 15

The power of the motor is equal to the rate of increase of GPE of the mass, and is also given by current multiplied by voltage:

$$P = mgu = IV$$

$$I = \frac{mgu}{V} = \frac{100 \times 10 \times 0.5}{230} = \frac{50}{23} \text{ A}$$

Due to the configuration of the pulley with three strings, the linear velocity of the string connected to the winding reel is $3u$. This is related to the angular velocity of the winding reel by

$$v = r\omega$$

$$\omega = \frac{v}{r} = \frac{3u}{D/2} = \frac{3 \times 0.5}{0.05/2} = 60 \text{ rad/s}$$

The force of the motor is related to power and velocity by

$$P = Fv$$

$$F = \frac{P}{v} = \frac{mug}{3u} = \frac{mg}{3} = \frac{100 \times 10}{3} = \frac{1000}{3} \approx 333.3 \text{ N}$$

Question 16

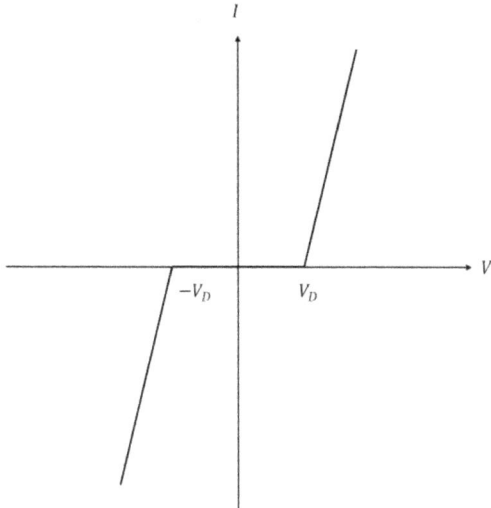

The voltage drop-off, V_D, is approximately 0.7 V, below which no current is generated.

During normal operation, where the voltage is in the range $-V_D$ to V_D, no current will pass through C-D and the amplifier will operate as normal. When there is a discharge and a high voltage ($> V_D$) is applied, current is diverted through C-D and so the amplifier is protected.

Question 17

Let the smaller mass have speed v_1, and the larger mass be v_2. Consider conservation of momentum:

$$mv_1 + 2mv_2 = 0$$

$$v_1 = -2v_2$$

At maximum speed, all electrostatic potential energy must have been converted to kinetic energy:

$$k\frac{(Q)(2Q)}{d} = \frac{1}{2}mv_1^2 + \frac{1}{2}(2m)v_2^2$$

$$\frac{4kQ^2}{d} = m(-2v_2)^2 + 2mv_2^2 = 6mv_2^2$$

$$v_2 = \sqrt{\frac{4kQ^2}{6md}} = Q\sqrt{\frac{2k}{3md}}$$

Question 18

a) When a wave travels from a more optically dense medium to a less optically dense medium, refraction occurs and the wave bends away from the normal. At a critical angle, θ_c, as shown in the diagram below, the angle of refraction has reached 90°. At angles of incidence above this critical angle, total internal reflection occurs where the wave is entirely reflected from the boundary.

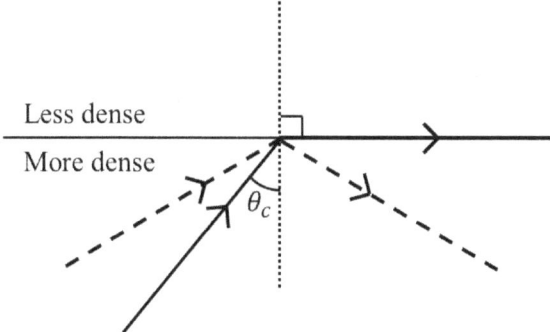

b) The angle of refraction is related to the angle of incidence by Snell's law: $n_1 \sin \theta_1 = n_2 \sin \theta_2$. Since the angle of refraction is equal to 90° at the critical angle,

$$n_1 \sin \theta_c = n_2 \sin 90$$

$$\theta_c = \sin^{-1}\left(\frac{n_2}{n_1}\right)$$

c)

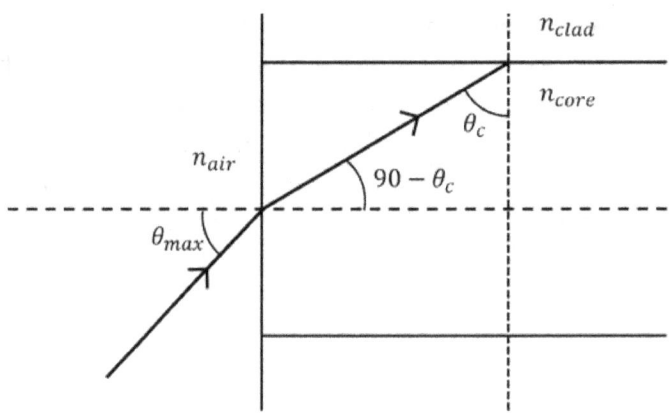

For light to be transmitted along the fibre, every angle of incidence at an interface between the core and cladding must be greater than or equal to the critical angle, so that total internal reflection occurs and no light refracts out. If the initial angle of incidence increases beyond θ_{max}, the angle of incidence at the interface between the core and cladding will decrease below the critical angle. Consider the core-cladding interface:

$$\sin \theta_c = \frac{n_{clad}}{n_{core}} \quad (1)$$

Now consider the air-core interface:

$$n_{air} \sin \theta_{max} = n_{core} \sin(90 - \theta_c)$$

$$\sin \theta_{max} = \frac{n_{core}}{n_{air}} \cos \theta_c$$

$$\sin \theta_{max} = \frac{n_{core}}{n_{air}} \sqrt{1 - \sin^2 \theta_c}$$

Substitute equation (1) in:

$$\sin\theta_{max} = \frac{n_{core}}{n_{air}}\sqrt{1 - \left(\frac{n_{clad}}{n_{core}}\right)^2}$$

$$\sin\theta_{max} = \frac{\sqrt{n_{core}^2 - n_{clad}^2}}{n_{air}}$$

$$\theta_{max} = \sin^{-1}\left[\frac{\sqrt{n_{core}^2 - n_{clad}^2}}{n_{air}}\right]$$

d) Since water has a higher refractive index than air, when entering the water tank the light will bend towards the normal, with angle θ_w as shown. The light will leave the water tank at an angle of θ_a, which is then parallel to the original edge of the beam. Hence, the circular spot will be smaller:

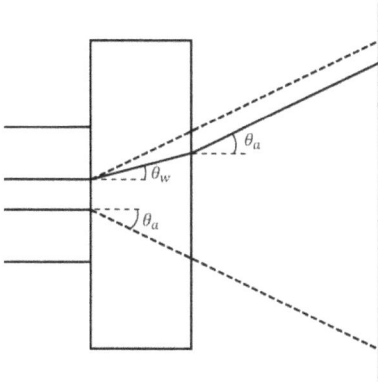

e) As refractive index changes with wavelength, the image will now be a white central spot with a rainbow around it.

Question 19

a) A sketch of the system with all forces is shown below:

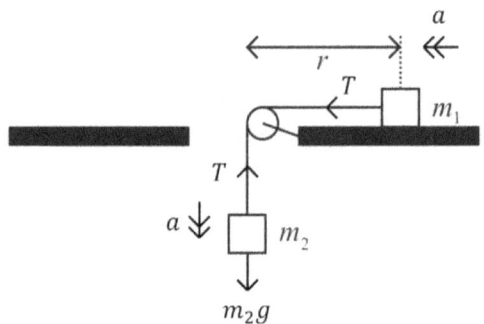

Consider the first mass using Newton's second law:

$$T = m_1 a \quad (1)$$

Similarly, consider the second mass:

$$m_2 g - T = m_2 a$$

$$T = m_2 a + m_2 g \quad (2)$$

$$m_2 g - T = m_2 a$$

$$T = m_2 g - m_2 a \quad (2)$$

Set the two equations equal to each other:

$$m_1 a = m_2 a + m_2 g$$

$$m_1 a = m_2 a + m_2 g$$

$$a = \frac{m_2 g}{m_1 + m_2}$$

Substitute back into (1):

$$T = \frac{m_1 m_2 g}{m_1 + m_2}$$

b) The system is now as shown below, where $F_{fr} = \mu_s m_1 g$ if the masses are stationary, or $F_{fr} = \mu_d m_1 g$ if the system is moving.

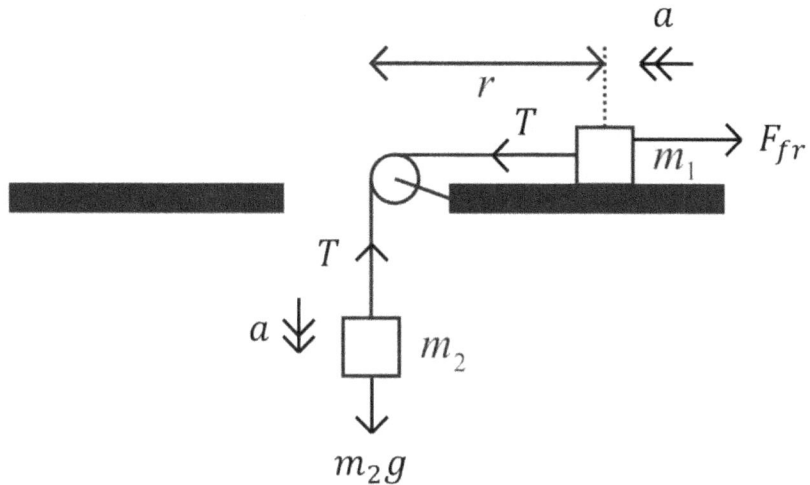

Assuming the masses start from rest, there are two possible scenarios, where $a = 0$ and where $a > 0$. When $a = 0$, $T = m_2 g$ and the system is in equilibrium. However, when $a > 0$ and the system is moving, consider each mass in turn as before. For m_1,

$$T - \mu_d m_1 g = m_1 a$$

$$T = \mu_d m_1 g + m_1 a \quad (1)$$

Similarly, for m_2,

$$m_2 g - T = m_2 a$$

$$T = m_2 g - m_2 a \quad (2)$$

Set (1) equal to (2):

$$\mu_d m_1 g + m_1 a = m_2 g - m_2 a$$

$$a = \frac{g(m_2 - \mu_d m_1)}{m_1 + m_2}$$

$$T = m_2 g - \frac{m_2 g(m_2 - \mu_d m_1)}{m_1 + m_2}$$

$$T = g \frac{(m_1 m_2 + m_2^2) - (m_2^2 - \mu_d m_1 m_2)}{m_1 + m_2} = \frac{g m_1 m_2 (1 + \mu_d)}{m_1 + m_2}$$

For m_1 to accelerate, tension must be greater than static friction on the first mass, but tension must also be less than the weight of m_2. Therefore $T > \mu_s m_1 g$ and $T < m_2 g$:

$$\mu_s m_1 g < T < m_2 g$$

$$\boldsymbol{\mu_s m_1 < m_2}$$

c) At r_{min}, m_2 is about to accelerate down, so friction acts outwards:

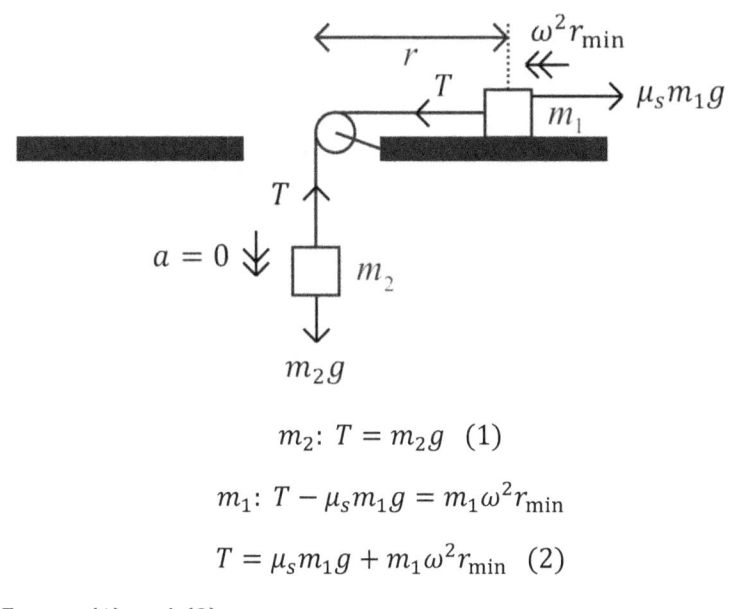

$$m_2: \quad T = m_2 g \quad (1)$$

$$m_1: \quad T - \mu_s m_1 g = m_1 \omega^2 r_{min}$$

$$T = \mu_s m_1 g + m_1 \omega^2 r_{min} \quad (2)$$

Equate (1) and (2):

$$m_2 g = \mu_s m_1 g + m_1 \omega^2 r_{min}$$

$$\boldsymbol{r_{min} = \frac{g(m_2 - \mu_s m_1)}{m_1 \omega^2}}$$

At r_{max}, m_2 is about to accelerate upwards, so friction acts inwards:

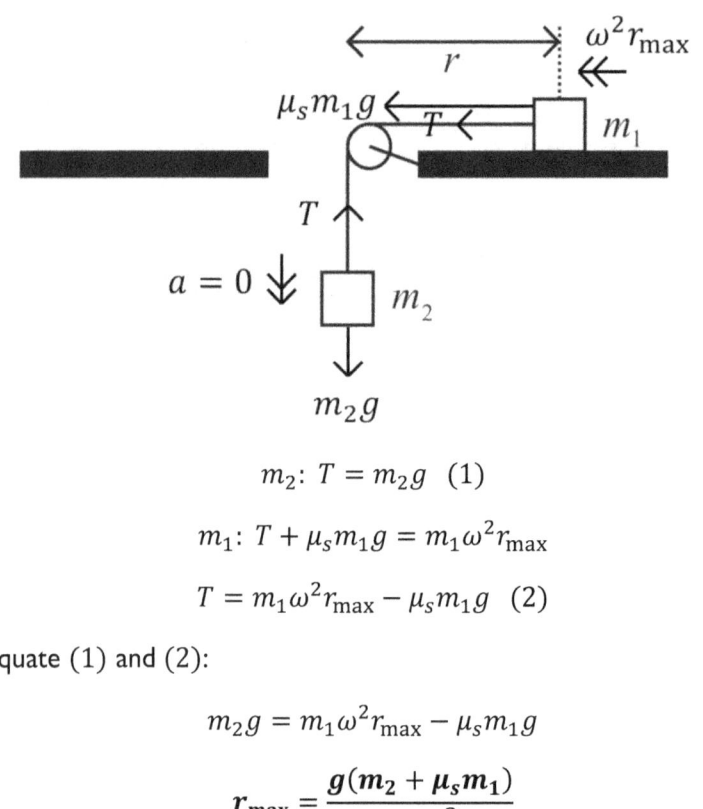

m_2: $T = m_2 g$ (1)

m_1: $T + \mu_s m_1 g = m_1 \omega^2 r_{max}$

$T = m_1 \omega^2 r_{max} - \mu_s m_1 g$ (2)

Equate (1) and (2):

$$m_2 g = m_1 \omega^2 r_{max} - \mu_s m_1 g$$

$$r_{max} = \frac{g(m_2 + \mu_s m_1)}{m_1 \omega^2}$$

END OF PAPER

2015

PART A

Question 1

Using Pascal's Triangle, the expansion is

$$(2x + x^2)^5 = (2x)^5 + (5)(2x)^4(x^2) + (10)(2x)^3(x^2)^2$$
$$+ 10(2x)^2(x^2)^3 + (5)(2x)(x^2)^4 + (x^2)^5$$
$$= 32x^5 + 80x^6 + 80x^7 + 40x^8 + 10x^9 + x^{10}$$

Question 2

$$\log_2 x + \log_4 16 = 2$$
$$\log_2 x + 2 = 2$$
$$\log_2 x = 0$$
$$x = 2^0 = 1$$

Question 3

This is a geometric series with first term $a = \frac{1}{3}$ and common ratio $r = \frac{1}{3}$. Hence,

$$S_n = \frac{a(1-r^n)}{1-r} = \frac{\frac{1}{3}\left(1-\left(\frac{1}{3}\right)^5\right)}{1-\frac{1}{3}} = \frac{\frac{1}{3} \times \left(1 - \frac{1}{243}\right)}{2/3} = \frac{1}{2} \times \frac{242}{243} = \frac{121}{243}$$

$$S_\infty = \frac{a}{1-r} = \frac{\frac{1}{3}}{1-\frac{1}{3}} = \frac{1}{2}$$

Question 4

Let $u = (x-4)(x-2) = x^2 - 6x + 8$. Then $\frac{du}{dx} = 2x - 6$. Also, when $x = 6$, $u = 8$ and when $x = 4$, $u = 0$. Substitute these into the integral:

$$\int_4^6 (2x-6)[(x-4)(x-2)]^{1/2} dx = \int_0^8 u^{1/2} du$$

$$= \left[\frac{2}{3} u^{\frac{3}{2}}\right]_0^8 = \frac{2}{3}(\sqrt{8})^3 = \frac{2}{3}(2\sqrt{2})^3 = \frac{2}{3}(8)(2\sqrt{2}) = \frac{32\sqrt{2}}{3}$$

Question 5

$$4x^2 + 8x - 8 = m(4x - 3)$$

$$4x^2 + 8x - 8 - 4mx + 3m = 0$$

$$4x^2 + (8 - 4m)x + (3m - 8) = 0$$

This is now a quadratic in x of the form $ax^2 + bx + c = 0$. There are no real solutions when $b^2 - 4ac < 0$. Therefore,

$$(8 - 4m)^2 - 4(4)(4m - 8) < 0$$

$$64 - 64m + 16m^2 - 64m + 128 < 0$$

$$16m^2 - 128m + 192 < 0$$

$$m^2 - 8m + 12 < 0$$

$$(m - 3)(m - 4) < 0$$

$$3 < m < 4$$

Question 6

a) The possible scenarios are TTH, HTT and TTT. Each scenario has an individual probability of $\frac{1}{2} \times \frac{1}{2} \times \frac{1}{2} = \frac{1}{8}$. Hence, the total probability of two or more tails in succession is $3 \times \frac{1}{8} = \frac{3}{8}$.

b) Two consecutive tosses being the same can either have the outcome HH or TT. Each has a probability of $\frac{1}{2} \times \frac{1}{2} = \frac{1}{4}$, and so the total probability is $2 \times \frac{1}{4} = \frac{1}{2}$.

c) The probability than any one of the tosses is a tail is

$$P(T \geq 1) = 1 - P(H = 3) = 1 - \frac{1}{8} = \frac{7}{8}$$

The probability that all tosses resulted in tails is $\frac{1}{2} \times \frac{1}{2} \times \frac{1}{2} = \frac{1}{8}$. Hence the probability that all tosses are tails given that at least one toss is a tail is

$$\frac{1/8}{7/8} = \frac{1}{7}$$

Question 7

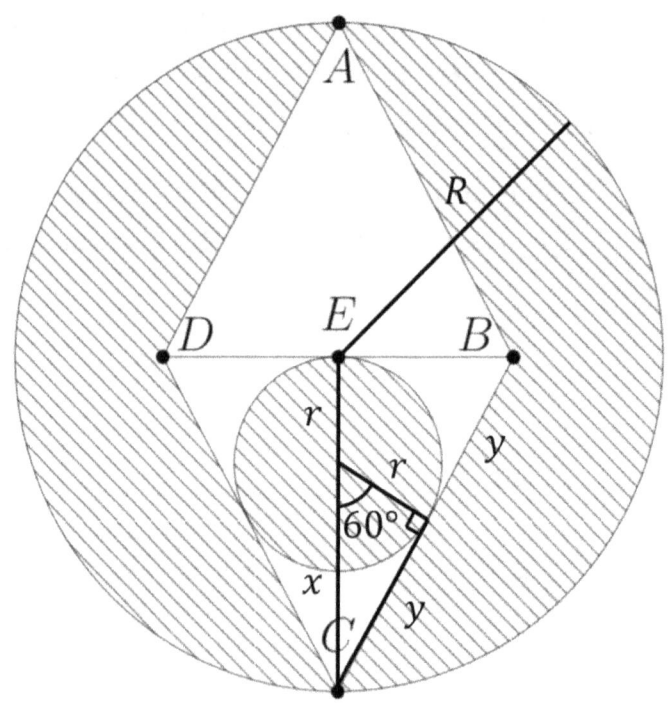

Considering the right-angled triangle in the sketch above,

$$\frac{r}{x} = \cos 60 = \frac{1}{2}$$

$$x = 2r \quad (1)$$

$$\frac{y}{r} = \tan 60 = \sqrt{3}$$

$$y = \sqrt{3}r \quad (2)$$

$$R = x + r = 3r \quad (3)$$

Area of triangle DCB: $A_{\text{DCB}} = \frac{1}{2}(2y)R = \frac{1}{2}(2\sqrt{3}r)(3r) = 3\sqrt{3}r^2$.

Area of big circle: $A_{\text{big}} = \pi R^2 = \pi(3r)^2 = 9\pi r^2$

Area of small circle: $A_{\text{small}} = \pi r^2$.

The shaded area is therefore given by

$$A = A_{\text{big}} - 2A_{\text{DCB}} + A_{\text{small}}$$

$$= 9\pi r^2 - 2(3\sqrt{3}r^2) + \pi r^2 = 10\pi r^2 - 6\sqrt{3}r^2 = \mathbf{2r^2(5\pi - 3\sqrt{3})}$$

Question 8

This is a circle with centre $(-3, 3)$ and radius $\sqrt{17}$:

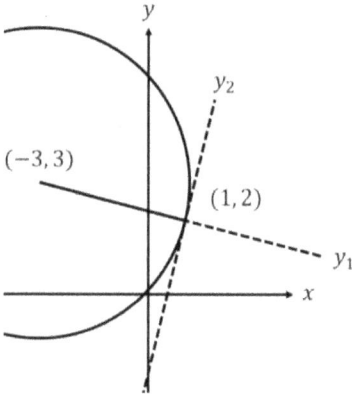

The gradient of the line connecting the centre of the circle to the point $(1, 2)$ is

$$m_1 = \frac{2 - 3}{1 - (-3)} = -\frac{1}{4}$$

The gradient of the line that is normal to the circle, y_1, is therefore $-\frac{1}{4}$.

The gradient of the line that is tangent to the circle, y_2, is

$$m_2 = -\frac{1}{m_1} = 4$$

Therefore, the equation of the normal is

$$y - 2 = -\frac{1}{4}(x - 1)$$

$$y = -\frac{1}{4}x + \frac{9}{4}$$

The normal therefore has a y-intercept of $\frac{9}{4}$. The equation of the tangent is

$$y - 2 = 4(x - 1)$$

$$y = 4x - 2$$

Therefore the y-intercept of the tangent is -2.

Question 9

First, consider what happens to the function as $x \to \pm\infty$:

As $x \to \infty$, $y \to -3$ from below.

As $x \to -\infty$, $y \to -3$ from below.

Asymptotes must exist where the denominator of the fraction is zero:

$$x^2 - 4 = 0$$

$$x = \pm 2$$

When $x = 0$, $y = -\frac{8}{-4} - 3 = -1$.

Finally, differentiate the function to find any turning points:

$$y = -8(x^2 - 4)^{-1} - 3$$

$$\frac{dy}{dx} = 8(2x)(x^2 - 4)^{-2} = 0$$

Therefore $x = 0$ (Since $(x^2 - 4)^{-2} = 0$ has no solutions). Hence, the sketch of the function is below:

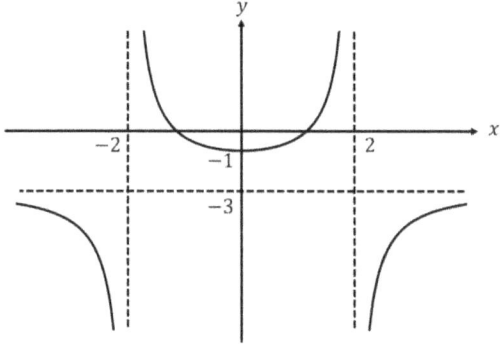

The range of y is therefore

$$\{y \geq -1\} \cup \{y < -3\}$$

PAT PAST PAPER SOLUTIONS — 2015

Question 10

Split these inequalities into two and multiply by $(x-6)^2$ as it is always positive:

$$-1(x-6)^2 < (3x+4)(x-6) \quad (1)$$

AND

$$(3x+4)(x-6) < (x-6)^2 \quad (2)$$

(1):

$$-x^2 + 12x - 36 < 3x^2 - 14x - 24$$

$$0 < 4x^2 - 26x + 12$$

$$0 < 2x^2 - 13x + 6$$

$$0 < (2x-1)(x-6)$$

$$x < \frac{1}{2} \text{ or } x > 6$$

(2):

$$3x^2 - 14x - 24 < x^2 - 12x + 36$$

$$2x^2 - 2x - 60 < 0$$

$$x^2 - x - 30 < 0$$

$$(x-6)(x+5) < 0$$

$$-5 < x < 6$$

Hence, combining the two inequalities gives $-5 < x < \frac{1}{2}$

END OF SECTION

PART B

Question 11

The initial vertical velocity of the ball is $10 \sin 30 = 5$ ms^{-1}. Consider the vertical motion of the ball, taking upwards as positive:

$$s = ut + \frac{1}{2}at^2$$

$$-10 = 5t + \frac{1}{2}(-10)t^2$$

$$-10 = 5t - 5t^2$$

$$t^2 - t - 2 = 0$$

$$(t-2)(t+1) = 0$$

Since $t > 0$,

$$t = 2 \text{ s}$$

Question 12

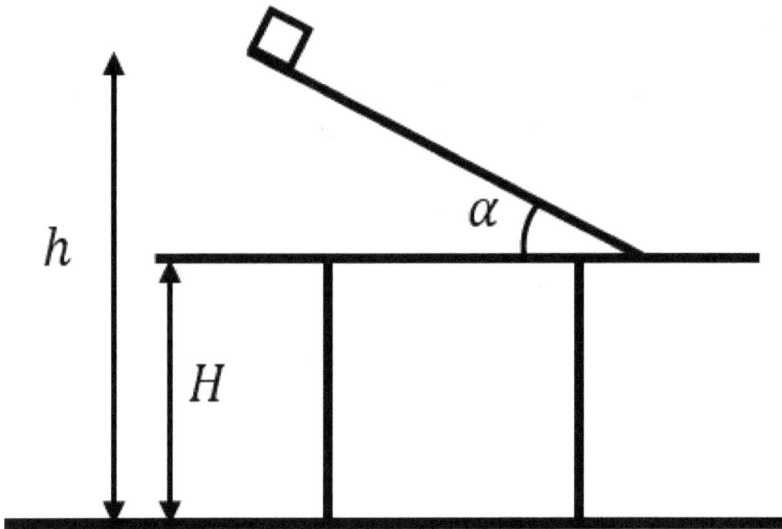

The height of the slope is $h - H$. Hence, the vertical distance travelled by the cube when it is halfway down is $\frac{h-H}{2}$.

Using conservation of energy, gravitational potential energy is converted into kinetic energy as the cube slides down the slope:

$$\frac{1}{2}mv^2 = mg\left(\frac{h-H}{2}\right)$$

$$v = \sqrt{g(h-H)}$$

Question 13

A solar eclipse occurs when the Moon completely blocks the view of the Sun from a point on Earth.

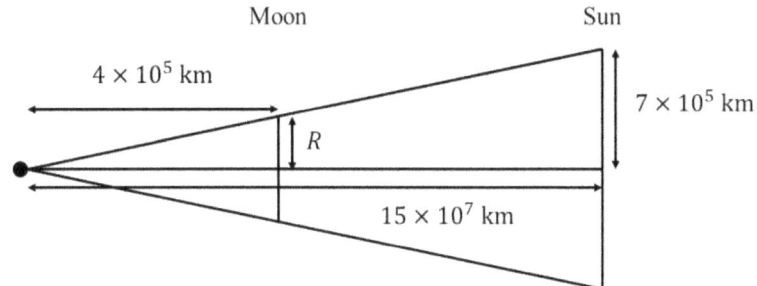

Using similar triangles,

$$\frac{R}{7 \times 10^5} = \frac{4 \times 10^5}{15 \times 10^7}$$

$$R = \frac{28 \times 10^{10}}{15 \times 10^7} = \frac{28000}{15} \approx \mathbf{1900 \text{ km}}$$

Question 14

The path of the ray of light is shown below:

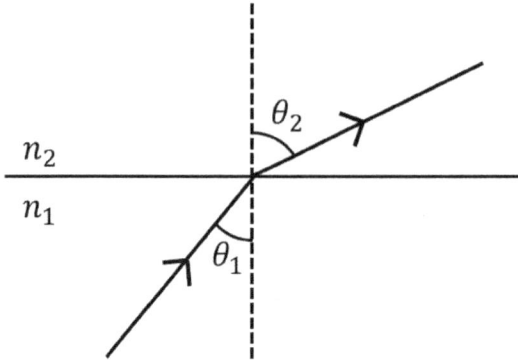

The angles are related by

$$n_1 \sin \theta_1 = n_2 \sin \theta_2$$

Light can only be completely reflected at the boundary when travelling into a region with a lower refractive index, so $n_1 > n_2$.

The critical angle of incidence occurs when the angle of refraction is 90°:

$$n_1 \sin \theta_c = n_2 \sin 90$$

$$\theta_c = \sin^{-1}\left(\frac{n_2}{n_1}\right)$$

Hence, complete reflection occurs when the angle of incidence is greater than this critical angle, so

$$\theta_1 > \sin^{-1}\left(\frac{n_2}{n_1}\right)$$

Question 15

As the mass does not move, all forces must be in equilibrium. First, resolve forces in the x direction:

$$A = C \cos 45 = \frac{C}{\sqrt{2}}$$

$$C = \sqrt{2}A$$

Now, resolve forces in the y direction:

$$B = C \sin 45 = \sqrt{2}A \times \frac{1}{\sqrt{2}}$$

$$\boldsymbol{B = A}$$

Question 16

Let the velocity of the 2 kg mass after the collision be v_2, and the velocity of the 1 kg mass after the collision be v_1.

Considering conservation of momentum,

$$2v_2 + v_1 = 2$$

$$v_1 = 2(1 - v_2) \quad (1)$$

Since the collision is elastic, energy must be conserved:

$$\frac{1}{2} \times 2 \times 1^2 = \frac{1}{2} \times 2 \times v_2^2 + \frac{1}{2} \times 1 \times v_1^2$$

$$2v_2^2 + v_1^2 = 2 \quad (2)$$

Substitute (1) into (2):

$$2v_2^2 + \left(2(1 - v_2)\right)^2 = 2$$

$$v_2^2 + 2(1 - 2v_2 + v_2^2) = 1$$

$$3v_2^2 - 4v_2 + 1 = 0$$

$$(3v_2 - 1)(v_2 - 1)$$

$$v_2 = 1 \text{ or } v_2 = \frac{1}{3}$$

The solution of $v_2 = 1$ is where the balls do not actually collide, so $v_2 = \frac{1}{3}$ ms^{-1}. Using equation (1),

$$v_1 = 2\left(1 - \frac{1}{3}\right) = \frac{4}{3} \text{ ms}^{-1}$$

Question 17

The vertical velocity is given by $\frac{dy}{dt}$:

$$\frac{dy}{dt} = -\omega A \cos(kx - \omega t)$$

Since $|\cos(kx - \omega t)| \leq 1$, $\frac{dy}{dt}_{max} = \omega A$. Since the amplitude of the waves is 0.5 m, $A = 0.5$. ω is given by

$$\omega = \frac{2\pi}{T} = 2\pi f = 2\pi \left(\frac{v}{\lambda}\right) = 2\pi \left(\frac{2}{10}\right) = \frac{2\pi}{5}$$

Hence, the maximum vertical velocity of the boat is

$$\frac{2\pi}{5} \times 0.5 = \frac{\pi}{5} \text{ ms}^{-1}$$

Question 18

a) The speed of the water is equal to the volume flow rate divided by the cross-sectional area:

$$v = \frac{x}{A}$$

b) In a time δt, a mass of $\rho x \delta t$ of water hits the wall, which has momentum of

$$p = \rho x \delta t \times v = \frac{\rho x^2 \delta t}{A}$$

The force on the wall is then given by $F = \frac{dp}{dt}$.

i) All of the momentum is lost, so

$$F = \left(\frac{\rho x^2 \delta t}{A} - 0\right) \bigg/ \delta t = \frac{\rho x^2}{A}$$

ii) The water rebounds with the same momentum but in the opposite direction:

$$F = \left(\frac{\rho x^2 \delta t}{A} + \frac{\rho x^2 \delta t}{A}\right) \bigg/ \delta t = \frac{2\rho x^2}{A}$$

Question 19

For a circular orbit, the gravitational force is equal to the centripetal force:

$$\frac{GMm}{r^2} = \frac{mv^2}{r}$$

$$v^2 = \frac{GM}{r}$$

$$v = \sqrt{\frac{GM}{r}}$$

The acceleration due to gravity is given by $\frac{GM}{r^2}$, so

$$g = \frac{GM}{r^2}$$

$$\frac{GM}{r} = gr = 10 \times 6400 \times 10^3 = 64 \times 10^6$$

Hence,

$$v = \sqrt{\frac{GM}{r}} = \sqrt{64 \times 10^6} = \mathbf{8000 \text{ ms}^{-1}}$$

It would be difficult for a satellite to maintain a circular orbit around the equator at sea level, however, as the Earth's radius is not constant, and the satellite may come across obstructions such as mountains.

Question 20

For any energy change from level a to level b, the energy released is given by

$$\Delta E_{a,b} = -\left(\frac{R}{a^2}\right) - \left(-\frac{R}{b^2}\right) = R\left(\frac{1}{b^2} - \frac{1}{a^2}\right)$$

The largest energy release therefore comes when b is very low and a is very high. Similarly, the smallest energy release comes from when a and b are consecutive integers, and are both as high as possible.

$$\Delta E_{a,b} = \frac{R(a^2 - b^2)}{a^2 b^2}$$

Since $\Delta E = hf = \frac{hc}{\lambda}$,

$$\lambda_{a,b} = \frac{hc}{\Delta E_{a,b}} = \frac{hca^2 b^2}{R(a^2 - b^2)}$$

a) The shortest wavelength is emitted when a is as big as possible and b is as small as possible:

$$\lambda_{10,1} = \frac{hc(10^2)(1^2)}{R(10^2 - 1^2)} = \frac{100hc}{99R}$$

b) The longest wavelength is emitted when a and b are as close as possible (i.e. consecutive integers) but as large as possible:

$$\lambda_{10,9} = \frac{hc(10^2)(9^2)}{R(10^2 - 9^2)} = \frac{8100hc}{19R}$$

c) For every level, n, there are $n - 1$ possible emission lines. Hence, there are a total of

$$9 + 8 + 7 + \cdots + 2 + 1 = 45$$

Question 21

a) The resistance of the middle line of resistors is $2R$, and the resistance of the bottom line is $\frac{3R}{2}$. Hence, the total resistance between A and B is given by

$$\frac{1}{R_{AB}} = \frac{1}{R} + \frac{1}{2R} + \frac{2}{3R} = \frac{6+3+4}{6R} = \frac{13}{6R}$$

$$R_{AB} = \frac{6R}{13}$$

b) As the branches are in parallel, there will also be a potential difference of V across the bottom line of resistors. The voltage across the resistor between B and D is therefore given by

$$V_{BD} = \frac{R}{\left(\frac{3R}{2}\right)} V = \frac{2V}{3}$$

The power dissipated in the resistor is therefore given by

$$P_{BD} = \frac{V_{BD}^2}{R} = \frac{\left(\frac{2V}{3}\right)^2}{R} = \frac{4V^2}{9R}$$

c) It is easiest to redraw the resistor array as below:

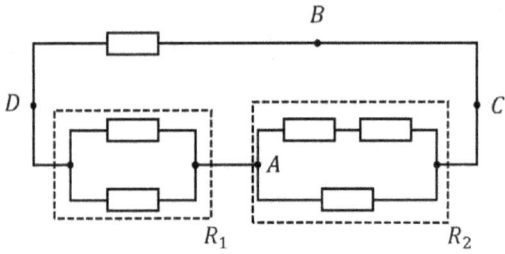

The resistance of R_1 is given by

$$\frac{1}{R_1} = \frac{1}{R} + \frac{1}{R} = \frac{2}{R}$$

$$R_1 = \frac{R}{2}$$

Similarly, R_2 is given by

$$\frac{1}{R_2} = \frac{1}{2R} + \frac{1}{R} = \frac{3}{2R}$$

$$R_2 = \frac{2R}{3}$$

Hence the resistance of the bottom line is $\frac{R}{2} + \frac{2R}{3} = \frac{3R+4R}{6} = \frac{7R}{6}$.

The total resistance between C and D is therefore

$$\frac{1}{R_{CD}} = \frac{1}{R} + \frac{6}{7R} = \frac{7+6}{7R} = \frac{13}{7R}$$

$$R_{CD} = \frac{7R}{13}$$

END OF PAPER

… PAT PAST PAPER SOLUTIONS | 2016

2016

PART A

Question 1

Let $y = x \sin x^2 = uv$, where $u = x$ and $v = \sin x^2$. Then $\frac{du}{dx} = 1$ and $\frac{dv}{dx} = 2x \cos x^2$. Now, apply the product rule:

$$\frac{dy}{dx} = v\frac{du}{dx} + u\frac{dv}{dx} = \sin x^2 + 2x^2 \cos x^2$$

Question 2

$$\sqrt{3} \tan^2 \theta - 2 \tan \theta - \sqrt{3} = 0$$

$$(\sqrt{3} \tan \theta + 1)(\tan \theta - \sqrt{3}) = 0$$

$$\tan \theta = -\frac{1}{\sqrt{3}} \text{ or } \tan \theta = \sqrt{3}$$

$$\theta = \frac{5\pi}{6}, \frac{11\pi}{6}, \frac{\pi}{3}, \frac{4\pi}{3}$$

Question 3

Consider the first equation:

$$\log_4\left(\frac{64^x}{16^y}\right) = 13$$

$$\log_4 64^x - \log_4 16^y = 13$$

$$\log_4 4^{3x} - \log_4 4^{2y} = 13$$

$$3x \log_4 4 - 2y \log_4 4 = 13$$

$$3x - 2y = 13 \quad (1)$$

Now consider the second equation:

$$\log_{10} 10^x + \log_3 3^y = 1$$

$$x \log_{10} 10 + y \log_3 3 = 1$$

$$x + y = 1$$

$$y = 1 - x$$

Substitute this into (1):

$$3x - 2(1-x) = 13$$

$$5x = 15$$

$$x = 3$$

$$y = -2$$

PAT PAST PAPER SOLUTIONS 2016

Question 4

The general formula for each term in the expansion is

$${}^{12}_nCx^n\left(-\frac{1}{x^2}\right)^{12-n}$$

The term independent of x will occur when the power that x is raised to is twice the power that $\left(-\frac{1}{x^2}\right)$ is raised to:

$$n = 2 \times (12 - n)$$

$$n = 24 - 2n$$

$$3n = 24$$

$$n = 8$$

Hence, the term independent of x is

$${}^{12}_8Cx^8\left(-\frac{1}{x^2}\right)^4 = {}^{12}_8C = \frac{12!}{(12-8)!\,(8!)} = \frac{12!}{4!\,8!} = \frac{12 \times 11 \times 10 \times 9}{4 \times 3 \times 2 \times 1}$$

$$= \frac{11 \times 10 \times 9}{2} = 11 \times 5 \times 9 = \mathbf{495}$$

Question 5

Firstly, consider 5-digit numbers. Any combination is greater than 5000, and so there are $5 \times 4 \times 3 \times 2 \times 1 = 120$ possible combinations.

Now, consider 4-digit numbers. All numbers beginning with 5, 6 or 7 will be valid. Hence, there are $3 \times 4 \times 3 \times 2 \times 1 = 72$ possible combinations.

In total, there are therefore $120 + 72 = \mathbf{192\ numbers}$.

Question 6

The number of new twigs and leaves each month is shown in the table below:

Month	0	1	2	3	...
New twigs	0	1	2	4	...
New leaves	0	2	3	8	...

Hence, the total number of leaves on the plant is given by a geometric series, with first term $a = 2$ and ration $r = 2$. The sum of the first 10 terms is

$$S_{10} = \frac{a(r^{10} - 1)}{r - 1} = \frac{2(2^{10} - 1)}{2 - 1} = 2 \times (1024 - 1) = \mathbf{2046}$$

Question 7

The required sequence is 6,5,4,3,3,3,3,2,2,1 (10 throws).

a) If the die is only thrown 8 times, it is impossible to achieve the sequence of 10 digits, and so the probability is **zero**.

b) For 10 throws, each number must be exactly right, so the probability is $\left(\frac{1}{6}\right)^{10}$.

c) For 12 throws, there are three possible scenarios:

$$\langle\text{sequence}\rangle xx, \quad x\langle\text{sequence}\rangle x, \quad xx\langle\text{sequence}\rangle$$

In each of these cases, x can take 6 different values and so there are 6^2 different combinations of each option. Since there are 6^{12} possible combinations from 12 dice rolls, the probability of winning is

$$\frac{3 \times 6^2}{6^{12}} = \frac{3}{6^{10}}$$

PAT PAST PAPER SOLUTIONS 2016

Question 8

Consider the octagon as shown below, with a right-angled triangle in each corner:

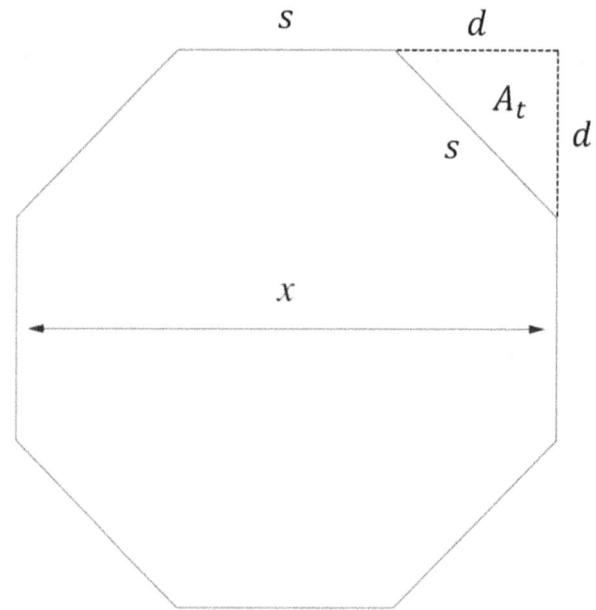

Using Pythagoras' theorem, $2d^2 = s^2 \rightarrow d = \frac{s}{\sqrt{2}}$. The area of the triangle is therefore $A_t = \frac{1}{2} \times d^2 = \frac{s^2}{4}$. Considering the width of the whole shape,

$$s + 2\frac{s}{\sqrt{2}} = x$$

$$s(1 + \sqrt{2}) = x$$

$$s = \frac{x}{1 + \sqrt{2}}$$

~ 220 ~

The area of the octagon is therefore given by

$$A_{oct} = x^2 - 4A_t = x^2 - s^2$$

$$A_{oct} = x^2 - \left(\frac{x}{1+\sqrt{2}}\right)^2 = x^2 \left(\frac{(1+\sqrt{2})^2 - 1}{(1+\sqrt{2})^2}\right) = x^2 \left(\frac{2+2\sqrt{2}}{(1+\sqrt{2})^2}\right)$$

$$A_{oct} = \frac{2x^2}{1+\sqrt{2}}$$

Setting the area of each shape equal to each other therefore gives

$$\frac{2x^2}{1+\sqrt{2}} = \pi r^2$$

$$x = r\sqrt{\frac{\pi(1+\sqrt{2})}{2}}$$

Question 9

Multiplying both sides by x^2 (as it is always positive):

$$5x^2 - 3x^3 < 2x$$

$$0 < x(3x^2 - 5x + 2)$$

$$0 < x(3x - 2)(x - 1)$$

Consider a number line with the relevant points:

[Number line: $-$ for $x<0$, $+$ for $0<x<2/3$, $-$ for $2/3<x<1$, $+$ for $x>1$]

$$\left\{0 < x < \frac{2}{3}\right\} \cup \{x > 1\}$$

Question 10

A sketch of the curves is shown below:

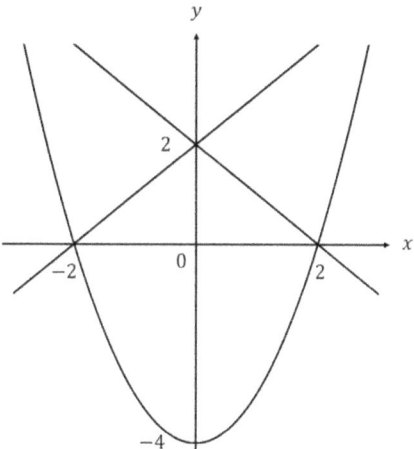

Since the enclosed area is symmetrical about the y-axis, it can be calculated by doubling the enclosed area between $x = 0$ and $x = 2$. This area is equal to the area between the line $y = 2 - x$ and the x-axis plus the area between the curve $y = x^2 - 4$ and the x-axis (given by the negative integral as the area is below the x-axis).

$$A = 2\left(\int_0^2 (2-x)\,dx - \int_0^2 (x^2 - 4)\,dx\right)$$

$$= 2\left(\left[2x - \frac{x^2}{2}\right]_0^2 - \left[\frac{x^3}{3} - 4x\right]_0^2\right)$$

$$= 2\left(4 - \frac{4}{2} - \frac{8}{3} + 8\right) = 2\left(10 - \frac{8}{3}\right) = 2 \times \frac{22}{3} = \frac{44}{3}$$

Question 11

Find $\frac{dr}{dt}$ using the chain rule:

$$\frac{dr}{dt} = \frac{dr}{dh} \times \frac{dh}{dt}$$

Since $h(t) = h_0 - \alpha t$, $\frac{dh}{dt} = -\alpha$.

As volume is constant,

$$V = \pi r^2 h = \text{constant}$$

$$r = \sqrt{\frac{V}{\pi h}} = \sqrt{\frac{V}{\pi}} h^{-\frac{1}{2}}$$

$$\frac{dr}{dh} = -\frac{1}{2}\sqrt{\frac{V}{\pi}} h^{-\frac{3}{2}}$$

Hence, using the equation for the chain rule given above,

$$\frac{dr}{dt} = -\frac{1}{2}\sqrt{\frac{V}{\pi}} h^{-\frac{3}{2}} \times -\alpha = \frac{\alpha}{2}\sqrt{\frac{V}{\pi h^3}} = \frac{\alpha}{2}\sqrt{\frac{V}{\pi(h_0 - \alpha t)^3}}$$

Since $t < \frac{h_0}{\alpha}$, $h_0 - \alpha t > 0$. Hence, as t increases, $(h_0 - \alpha t)$ will decrease and so $\frac{dr}{dt}$ **will increase with time.**

END OF SECTION

PART B

Question 12

Since gravitational energy is given by $GPE = mgh$, the height of the ball is proportional to its energy. Therefore, after each bounce, the height of the ball will be $\frac{3}{4}$ of its previous height. Let h_n be the height of the ball after the nth bounce:

$$h_1 = \frac{3}{4}$$

$$h_2 = \frac{9}{16} \left(> \frac{1}{4}\right)$$

$$h_3 = \frac{27}{64} \left(> \frac{1}{4}\right)$$

$$h_4 = \frac{81}{216} \left(> \frac{1}{4}\right)$$

$$h_5 = \frac{243}{1024} \left(< \frac{1}{4}\right)$$

Hence, it takes **5 bounces** to bounce no higher than 0.25 m.

Question 13

a) An ideal wire has no resistance:

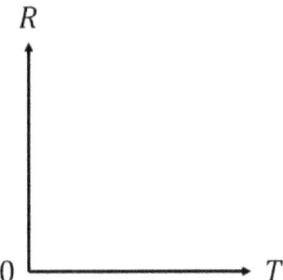

b) A filament light bulb's resistance increases with temperature, though not linearly:

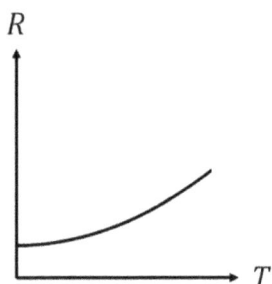

c) A thermistor's resistance decreases with temperature as follows:

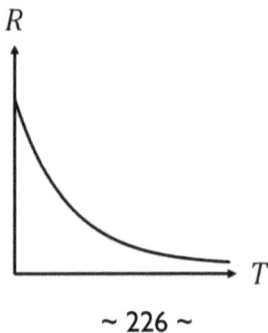

Question 14

Use Kepler's 3rd Law relating orbital period and radius:

$$T^2 \propto r^3$$

$$\left(\frac{T_E}{T_I}\right)^2 = \left(\frac{r_E}{r_I}\right)^3 = 1.6^3 = \left(\frac{16}{10}\right)^3$$

$$\frac{T_E}{T_I} = \left(\frac{16}{10}\right)^{\frac{3}{2}} = \left(\frac{4}{\sqrt{10}}\right)^3 = \frac{64}{10\sqrt{10}} = \frac{6.4}{\sqrt{10}}$$

Obtain an estimate for $\sqrt{10}$:

$3^2 = 9$ and $4^2 = 16$, so $\sqrt{10}$ must be slightly larger than 3.

$$3.1^2 = (3 + 0.1)^2 = 9 + 0.6 + 0.01 = 9.61 < 10$$

$$3.2^2 = (3 + 0.2)^2 = 9 + 1.2 + 0.04 = 10.24 > 10$$

$$3.15^2 = (3 + 0.15)^2 = 9 + 0.9 + 0.0225 = 9.9225 < 10$$

Hence, $\sqrt{10} = 3.2$ to one decimal place:

$$\frac{T_E}{T_I} \approx \frac{6.4}{3.2} = \mathbf{2.0}$$

Question 15

To cross the 100 m river in 10 seconds, the rower's resultant velocity must be 10 ms^{-1} perpendicular to the river. The velocity diagram is shown below:

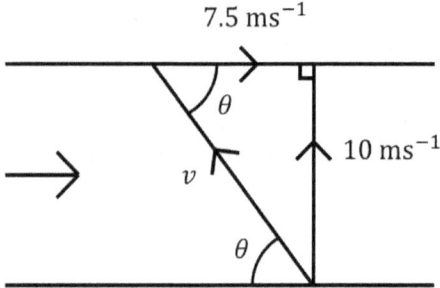

The triangle is proportional to a standard 3-4-5 right-angled triangle:

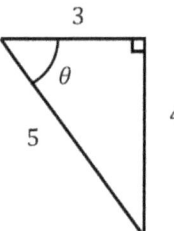

Hence, v is given by $5 \times \frac{10}{4} = 5 \times 2.5 = \mathbf{12.5 \text{ ms}^{-1}}$. θ is then given by

$$\tan \theta = \frac{4}{3}$$

$$\theta = \tan^{-1}\left(\frac{4}{3}\right)$$

Question 16

The force on $-q$ from a charge Q at a distance of r is given by

$$F = \frac{kQq}{r^2}$$

Hence,

$$F_1 = \frac{kQ_1 q}{x^2} \text{ and } F_2 = \frac{kQ_2 q}{(a-x)^2}$$

For there to be no net force,

$$F_1 = F_2$$

$$\frac{kQ_1 q}{x^2} = \frac{kQ_2 q}{(a-x)^2}$$

$$\frac{Q_1}{x^2} = \frac{Q_2}{(a-x)^2}$$

Let Q_2 be a multiple of Q_1, such that $Q_2 = mQ_1$:

$$\frac{Q_1}{x^2} = \frac{mQ_1}{(a-x)^2}$$

$$(a-x)^2 = mx^2$$

$$a^2 - 2ax + x^2 - mx^2 = 0$$

$$x^2(1-m) - 2ax + a^2 = 0$$

~ 229 ~

Use the quadratic formula:

$$x = \frac{-b \pm \sqrt{b^2 - 4ac}}{2a}$$

$$x = \frac{2a \pm \sqrt{(-2a)^2 - 4(1-m)(a^2)}}{2(1-m)}$$

$$= \frac{2a \pm \sqrt{4a^2 - 4a^2 + 4ma^2}}{2(1-m)}$$

$$x = \frac{2a \pm 2a\sqrt{m}}{2(1-m)} = \frac{a(1 \pm \sqrt{m})}{(1+\sqrt{m})(1-\sqrt{m})}$$

$$x = \frac{a}{1+\sqrt{m}} \text{ or } x = \frac{a}{1-\sqrt{m}}$$

Since $0 < x < a$,

$$x = \frac{a}{1+\sqrt{m}}$$

For the case where $Q_1 = Q_2$, $m = 1$ and so

$$x = \frac{a}{2}$$

When $Q_1 \neq Q_2$, $m = \frac{Q_2}{Q_1}$ and so

$$x = \frac{a}{1 + \sqrt{\frac{Q_2}{Q_1}}}$$

In this case, the unused solution $\left(x = \frac{a}{1-\sqrt{m}}\right)$ corresponds to a solution where either $x < 0$ or $x > a$ and so **the charge will lie outside Q_1 and Q_2**.

PAT PAST PAPER SOLUTIONS — 2016

Question 17

a) Work done is given by $\int F dx$, and so it is the area under the curve for a force-displacement diagram. Hence, the work done in moving the mass from $x = 5$ to $x = 0$ is $W = \frac{1}{2} \times 0.05 \times 10 = \mathbf{0.25 \, J}$.

b) Work done is converted to kinetic energy, so

$$\frac{1}{2}mv^2 = 0.25$$

$$v = \sqrt{\frac{2 \times 0.25}{0.02}} = \sqrt{25} = \mathbf{5 \, ms^{-1}}$$

c) The diagram shows that the relationship between force and displacement is $F = -kx$, where $k = 0.02$ from the graph. Hence, the acceleration is given by

$$m\frac{d^2x}{dt^2} = -kx$$

$$\frac{d^2x}{dt^2} = -\frac{k}{m}x = -\frac{0.02}{0.02}x = -x$$

This is therefore **simple harmonic motion**, where $\omega = 1 \, \text{rad/s}$. The period is $T = \frac{2\pi}{\omega} = 2\pi$ and the amplitude is 0.05 m.

~ 231 ~

Question 18

$$F = kr^x \eta^y v^z$$

Consider the SI units of each quantity:

$$[\text{kg m s}^{-2}] = [\text{m}]^x [\text{kg m}^{-1} \text{s}^{-1}]^y [\text{ms}^{-1}]^z$$

$$[\text{kg m s}^{-2}] = [\text{kg}]^y [\text{m}]^{x-y+z} [\text{s}]^{-y-z}$$

Equate the powers for each unit:

$$(\text{kg}): y = 1$$

$$(\text{s}): -y - z = -2$$

$$-1 - z = -2$$

$$z = 1$$

$$(\text{m}): x - y + z = 1$$

$$x - 1 + 1 = 1$$

$$x = 1$$

Question 19

a) Energy from the light is use to release the electron from the metal and also converted to kinetic energy of the electron:

$$hf = We + \frac{1}{2}mv^2$$

$$\frac{hc}{\lambda} = We + \frac{1}{2}mv^2$$

$$v^2 = \frac{2}{m}\left(\frac{hc}{\lambda} - We\right)$$

$$v^2 = \frac{2}{10^{-30}} \left(\frac{6 \times 10^{-34} \times 3 \times 10^8}{625 \times 10^{-9}} - 1 \times 1.6 \times 10^{-19} \right)$$

$$= 10^{30} \left(\frac{36 \times 10^{-26}}{6.25 \times 10^{-7}} - 3.2 \times 10^{-19} \right)$$

$$= 10^{30} \left(\frac{36}{6.25} \times 10^{-19} - 3.2 \times 10^{-19} \right)$$

$$= 10^{11} \left(\frac{144}{25} - \frac{16}{5} \right) = 10^{11} \left(\frac{144 - 80}{25} \right) = \frac{64}{25} \times 10^{11}$$

$$v = \frac{8}{5} \times 10^5 \times \sqrt{10} \approx 1.6 \times 3.2 \times 10^5 = \mathbf{5.1 \times 10^5 \ ms^{-1}}$$

b) The energy given to each electron is equal to Ae, where A is the accelerating voltage. Hence

$$KE_{final} = Ae + KE_{initial}$$

$$\frac{1}{2} m v_2^2 = Ae + \frac{1}{2} m v_1^2$$

$$\frac{1}{2} \times 10^{-30} v_2^2 = 5 \times 10^3 \times 1.6 \times 10^{-19} + \frac{1}{2} \times 10^{-30} \times \frac{64}{25} \times 10^{11}$$

$$10^{-30} v^2 = 10 \times 1.6 \times 10^{-16} + \frac{64}{25} \times 10^{-19}$$

$$10^{-30} v^2 \approx 10 \times 1.6 \times 10^{-16}$$

$$v^2 = 1.6 \times 10^{15} = 16 \times 10^{14}$$

$$v = \mathbf{4 \times 10^7 \ ms^{-1}}$$

Question 20

By symmetry, the potential difference across B is equal to the potential difference across C, as shown below:

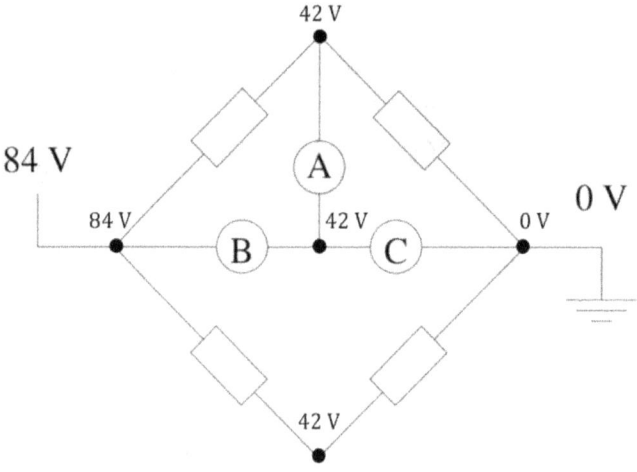

Similarly, the voltage at the node in the middle of each pair of resistors is also 42 V. Hence, there is no potential difference across A and so **heater A won't heat the water at all.**

The power dissipated in each heater is given by

$$P_B = P_C = \frac{V^2}{R} = \frac{42^2}{6} = 42 \times 7 = 294 \text{ W}$$

The energy required to heat each mass of water to 27°C is

$$E = mc\Delta T = 1 \times 4200 \times (27 - 7) = 7 \times 4200 \text{ J}$$

Hence, the time taken (which is the same for B and C) is

$$t = \frac{E}{P} = \frac{7 \times 4200}{7 \times 42} = 100 \text{ s}$$

Question 21

The diagram of the incident (and refracted) light can be drawn as follows:

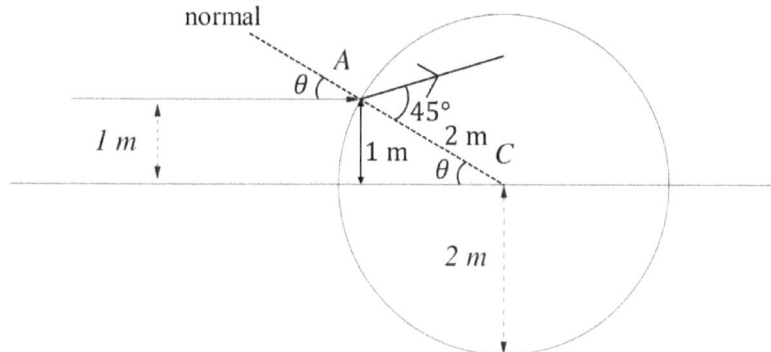

Considering the right-angled triangle formed inside the circle,

$$\sin\theta = \frac{1}{2}$$

Now consider the refractive index, n:

$$n_1 \sin\theta_1 = n_2 \sin\theta_2$$

$$n \sin\theta = \sin 45$$

$$\frac{n}{2} = \frac{\sqrt{2}}{2}$$

$$n = \sqrt{2}$$

For total internal reflection to occur, the angle of incidence must be greater than a certain critical angle, which is given by the point at which the angle of refraction is 90°:

$$n \sin \theta_c = \sin 90$$

$$\sin \theta_c = \frac{1}{n} = \frac{1}{\sqrt{2}}$$

$$\theta_c = 45°$$

Hence, the beam should be directed at an angle of **greater than 45°** to the line AC.

END OF PAPER

2017

Question 1: D

Use the product rule: $\frac{d}{dx}(uv) = v\frac{du}{dx} + u\frac{dv}{dx}$.

$$y = 2x \cos x$$

$$\frac{dy}{dx} = 2\cos x + 2x(-\sin x)$$

$$\frac{dy}{dx} = 2\cos x - 2x \sin x$$

Question 2: A

Divide both sides of the equation by 2 and then factorise:

$$2x^2 - 2x - 12 = 0$$

$$x^2 - x - 6 = 0$$

$$(x+2)(x-3) = 0$$

Question 3: E

This is a geometric series with $a = 1$ and $r = -e^{-1}$. However, the sum starts at $n = 0$ and so the first 11 terms are required to reach $n = 10$. The sum is therefore given by

$$S_{11} = \frac{a(1-r^{11})}{1-r}$$

$$= \frac{1-(-e^{-1})^{11}}{1-(-e^{-1})}$$

$$= \frac{1+e^{-11}}{1+e^{-1}}$$

$$\sim 237 \sim$$

PAT PAST PAPER SOLUTIONS 2017

Question 4: D

Collect terms with the same base and then take logs:

$$a^{3-x} b^{5x} = a^{x+5} b^{3x}$$

$$b^{5x-3x} = a^{x+5-(3-x)}$$

$$b^{2x} = a^{2x+2}$$

$$\log(b^{2x}) = \log(a^{2x+2})$$

$$2x \log b = (2x+2) \log a$$

$$x(\log b - \log a) = \log a$$

$$x = \frac{\log a}{\log b - \log a}$$

Question 5: B

Since the limits are symmetrical about the y-axis, integrating an odd function will give zero, as the area above and below the x-axis will cancel out. A function $f(x)$ is defined as odd if $f(-x) = -f(x)$. Using this definition, the functions in integrals I_1 **and** I_4 are odd and the integrals are therefore zero.

PAT PAST PAPER SOLUTIONS 2017

Question 6: C

It is clear that the graph has asymptotes at $x = -3$ and $x = 1$. The denominator of any possible function must therefore have roots at only $x = -3$ and $x = 1$. By inspection, options D and E are therefore excluded.

Option B can be factorised as

$$\frac{-1}{x^2 - 2x + 3} = \frac{-1}{(x-3)(x+1)}$$

The denominator has roots at $x = 3$ and $x = -1$ and so option B is excluded.

Option C can be factorised as

$$\frac{1}{x^2 + 2x - 3} = \frac{1}{(x+3)(x-1)}$$

The denominator has roots at $x = -3$ and $x = 1$ and so options A and C both have valid asymptotes. In option A, as $x \to -\infty, y < 0$ and so A is excluded. The valid function is therefore **option C**.

Question 7: C

The gravitational field on the Moon is weaker than that on the Earth but acts in exactly the same way, so the ball will fall back to the surface of the Moon.

Question 8: E

The electromagnetic spectrum from shortest to longest wavelength is: gamma ray, X-ray, ultraviolet, visible, infrared, microwave, radio.

Question 9: B

The overall resistance of the two resistors in parallel is given by

$$\frac{1}{R_p} = \frac{1}{R} + \frac{1}{2R} = \frac{3}{2R}$$

$$R_p = \frac{2R}{3}$$

The total resistance of the circuit is therefore

$$R_T = \frac{2R}{3} + R = \frac{5R}{3}$$

Using Ohm's law,

$$I = \frac{V}{R_T} = \frac{V}{5R/3} = \frac{3V}{5R}$$

Question 10: A

Capacitance is directly proportional to surface area. Therefore, if the area is halved, capacitance is also halved.

Question 11: B

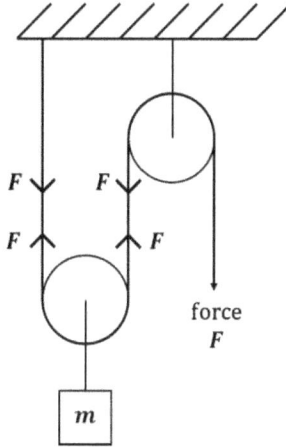

As the string is inextensible and the pulleys are frictionless, there must be a constant tension, F, throughout the string. Considering vertical equilibrium in the diagram above,

$$mg = 2F$$

$$F = \frac{mg}{2}$$

Question 12: A

The electric field strength is given by $E = \frac{V}{d}$ and the force on the charged particle is equal to $F = Eq$, hence $F = \frac{qV}{d}$. Since force is equal to the rate of change of momentum,

$$F = \frac{\Delta p}{\Delta t} = \frac{p_{initial}}{t} = \frac{qV}{d}$$

$$p_{initial} = \frac{qVt}{d}$$

Question 13

Use Pascal's triangle:

$$
\begin{array}{c}
1 \\
1 \quad 1 \\
1 \quad 2 \quad 1 \\
1 \quad 3 \quad 3 \quad 1 \\
1 \quad 4 \quad 6 \quad 4 \quad 1 \\
\boxed{1 \quad 5 \quad 10 \quad 10 \quad 5 \quad 1}
\end{array}
$$

$$(3+2x)^5 = 3^5 + 5(3)^4(2x) + 10(3)^3(2x)^2 + 10(3)^2(2x)^3$$
$$+ 5(3)(2x)^4 + (2x)^5$$

$$= \mathbf{243 + 810x + 1080x^2 + 720x^3 + 240x^4 + 32x^5}$$

Question 14

a) Since the probabilities of different people being busy are independent, the probability of all three people being busy is given by multiplying the individual probabilities:

$$P(\text{all busy}) = 0.5 \times 0.75 \times 0.2 = \mathbf{0.075}$$

b) Similarly, multiply the individual probabilities of not being busy:

$$P(\text{all free}) = (1 - 0.5) \times (1 - 0.75) \times (1 - 0.2)$$
$$= 0.5 \times 0.25 \times 0.8 = \mathbf{0.1}$$

PAT PAST PAPER SOLUTIONS | 2017

Question 15

To cause mass m to move, the elastic force from the spring must exceed the maximum static friction acting on mass m, given by $F_f = \mu_s mg$. Hence,

$$kx > \mu_s mg$$

$$x > \frac{\mu_s mg}{k}$$

Question 16

The volume of a cone is given by $V_c = \frac{\pi r_c^2 h_c}{3}$ and the volume of the sphere by $V_s = \frac{4}{3}\pi r^3$. Since $h_c = 2r$ and the volumes are equal,

$$\frac{\pi r_c^2 (2r)}{3} = \frac{4}{3}\pi r^3$$

$$r_c^2 = 2r^2$$

$$r_c = \sqrt{2}r$$

Question 17

Air resistance has units of $N(\equiv kgms^{-2})$:

$$\alpha \times [ms^{-1}]^2 \equiv kgms^{-2}$$

$$\alpha \equiv \frac{kgms^{-2}}{m^2s^{-2}} \equiv \mathbf{kgm^{-1}}$$

At terminal velocity, $\frac{dv}{dt} = 0$:

$$mg = \alpha v_t^2$$

$$v_t = \sqrt{\frac{mg}{\alpha}}$$

Consider conservation of energy:

$$W = GPE_{loss} - KE_{gain}$$

$$W = mgh - \frac{1}{2}mv_t^2 = mgh - \frac{1}{2}\frac{m^2 g}{\alpha}$$

$$W = mg\left(h - \frac{m}{2\alpha}\right)$$

Question 18

Since $\omega = 2\pi f$ and $v = f\lambda$,

$$v = \frac{\omega_1 \lambda_1}{2\pi} = \frac{\omega_2 \lambda_2}{2\pi}$$

$$y_1 + y_2 = A\left[\cos\left(\frac{2\pi x}{\lambda_1} - \omega_1 t\right) + \cos\left(\frac{2\pi x}{\lambda_2} - \omega_2 t\right)\right]$$

Using the formula given in the question,

$$y_1 + y_1 = 2A \cos\left(\pi x \left(\frac{1}{\lambda_1} + \frac{1}{\lambda_2}\right) - \frac{t(\omega_1 + \omega_2)}{2}\right) \cos\left(\pi x \left(\frac{1}{\lambda_1} - \frac{1}{\lambda_2}\right) + \frac{t(\omega_2 - \omega_1)}{2}\right)$$

$$= 2AC_1 C_2$$

Let the wavelength of C_1 be L_1 and the wavelength of C_2 be L_2:

$$\pi x \left(\frac{1}{\lambda_1} + \frac{1}{\lambda_2}\right) = \pi x \left(\frac{\lambda_1 + \lambda_2}{\lambda_1 \lambda_2}\right) = \frac{2\pi x}{L_1}$$

$$L_1 = \frac{2\lambda_1 \lambda_2}{\lambda_1 + \lambda_2}$$

Similarly,

$$L_2 = \frac{2\lambda_1 \lambda_2}{\lambda_2 - \lambda_1}$$

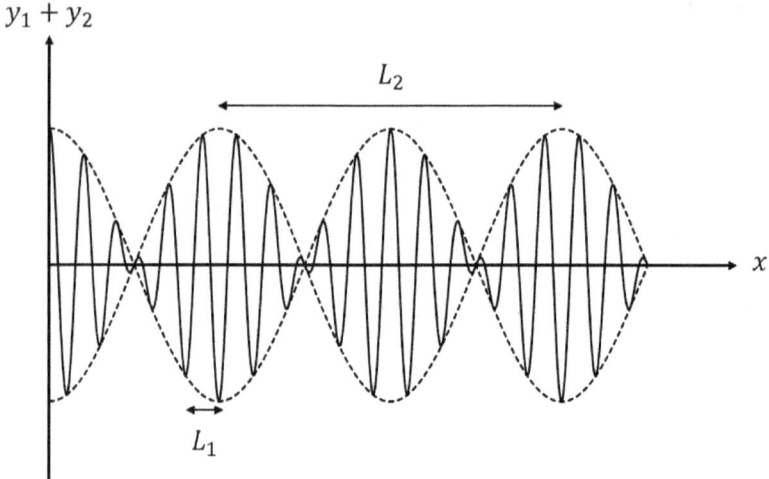

The frequency heard is given by

$$f = \frac{v}{\lambda} = \frac{v}{L_1} = \frac{\omega_1 \lambda_1}{2\pi}\left(\frac{\lambda_1 + \lambda_2}{2\lambda_1 \lambda_2}\right) = \frac{\omega_1(\lambda_1 + \lambda_2)}{4\pi\lambda_2}\left(= \frac{\omega_2(\lambda_1 + \lambda_2)}{4\pi\lambda_1}\right)$$

As shown on the graph, the distance between points where the sound disappears is

$$\frac{L_2}{2} = \frac{\lambda_1 \lambda_2}{\lambda_2 - \lambda_1}$$

Question 19

When $y = 0$,

$$a(\sqrt{3} - 2\cos\omega t) = 0$$

$$\cos\omega t = \frac{\sqrt{3}}{2}$$

$$\omega t = \frac{\pi}{6} + 2\pi n, \frac{11\pi}{6} + 2\pi n$$

where n is an integer. When $\omega t = \frac{\pi}{6} + 2\pi n$,

$$x = a\left(\frac{\pi}{6} + 2\pi n - \sin\left(\frac{\pi}{6} + 2\pi n\right)\right)$$

$$x = a\left(\frac{\pi}{6} + 2\pi n - \frac{1}{2}\right)$$

When $\omega t = \frac{11\pi}{6} + 2\pi n$,

$$x = a\left(\frac{11\pi}{6} + 2\pi n - \sin\left(\frac{11\pi}{6} + 2\pi n\right)\right)$$

$$x = a\left(\frac{11\pi}{6} + 2\pi n + \frac{1}{2}\right)$$

Question 20

Consider the first system with two stars:

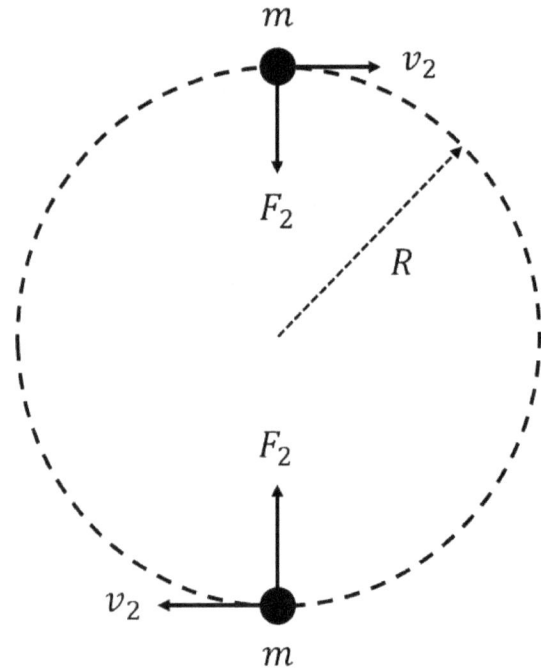

The gravitational force between the two stars must provide the centripetal force to keep each star in a circular orbit:

$$F_2 = \frac{Gmm}{(2R)^2} = \frac{mv_2^2}{R}$$

$$v_2^2 = \frac{Gm}{4R}$$

Now consider the second system:

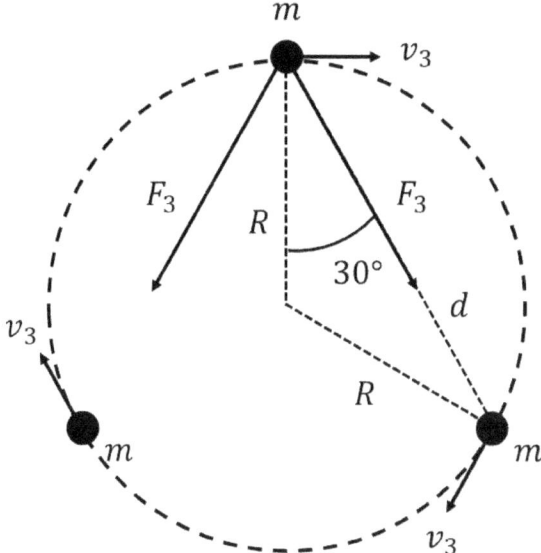

The gravitational forces between the stars must again provide the centripetal force, which acts perpendicular to each star's velocity:

$$2F_3 \cos 30 = \frac{mv_3^2}{R}$$

$$F_3 = \frac{mv_3^2}{\sqrt{3}R} \quad (1)$$

The distance between stars is given by

$$d = 2R \cos 30$$

$$d = \sqrt{3}R$$

The gravitational force is therefore

$$F_3 = \frac{Gmm}{\left(\sqrt{3}R\right)^2} \quad (2)$$

PAT PAST PAPER SOLUTIONS — 2017

Equating (1) and (2) gives

$$\frac{Gmm}{(\sqrt{3}R)^2} = \frac{mv_3^2}{\sqrt{3}R}$$

$$v_3^2 = \frac{Gm}{\sqrt{3}R}$$

Hence,

$$\frac{v_3^2}{v_2^2} = \frac{1/\sqrt{3}}{1/4} = \frac{4}{\sqrt{3}}$$

$$v_3 = \sqrt{\frac{4v_2^2}{\sqrt{3}}} = \frac{2v_2}{3^{\frac{1}{4}}}$$

Question 21

$$\frac{d}{dt}\int_0^{2t^2} (xt)^4\, dx = \frac{d}{dt}\int_0^{2t^2} x^4 t^4\, dx$$

$$= \frac{d}{dt}\left[\frac{t^4 x^5}{5}\right]_0^{2t^2} = \frac{d}{dt}\left[\frac{t^4(2t^2)^5}{5}\right] = \frac{d}{dt}\left[\frac{32t^{14}}{5}\right] = \frac{448t^{13}}{5}$$

Question 22

The equation of C_1 can be rewritten in standard form:
$$4x^2 + 24x + 4y^2 - 16y + 43 = 0$$
$$x^2 + 6x + y^2 - 4y + \frac{43}{4} = 0$$
$$(x+3)^2 - 9 + (y-2)^2 - 4 + \frac{43}{4} = 0$$
$$(x+3)^2 + (y-2)^2 = \left(\frac{3}{2}\right)^2$$

This is therefore a circle with centre $(-3, 2)$ and radius $\frac{3}{2}$. Similarly, C_2 can be written as

$$4x^2 - 40x + 4y^2 - 8y + 79 = 0$$
$$x^2 - 10x + y^2 - 2y + \frac{79}{4} = 0$$
$$(x-5)^2 - 25 + (y-1)^2 - 1 + \frac{79}{4} = 0$$
$$(x-5)^2 + (y-1)^2 = \left(\frac{5}{2}\right)^2$$

This is a circle with centre $(5, 1)$ and radius $\frac{5}{2}$. The sketch of the two circles and their tangents is shown below:

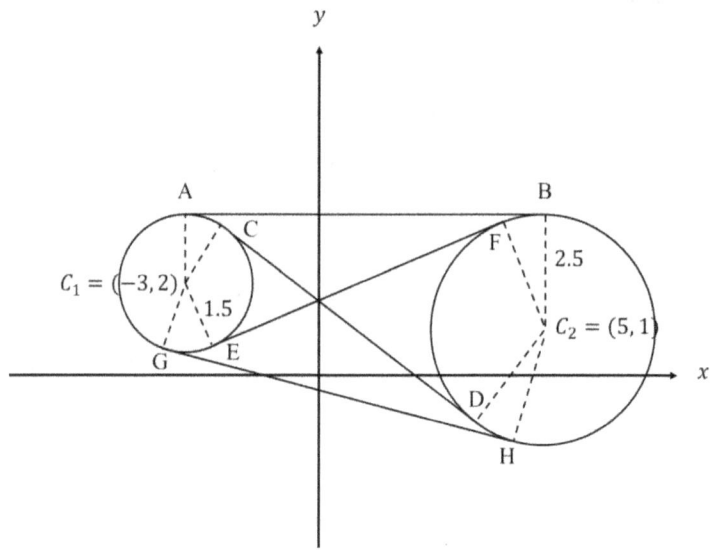

As it is horizontal, AB can be calculated as AB = 5 − (−3) = 8. By symmetry, **GH = AB = 8** and it is also clear that CD = EF. To find EF, consider the diagram below:

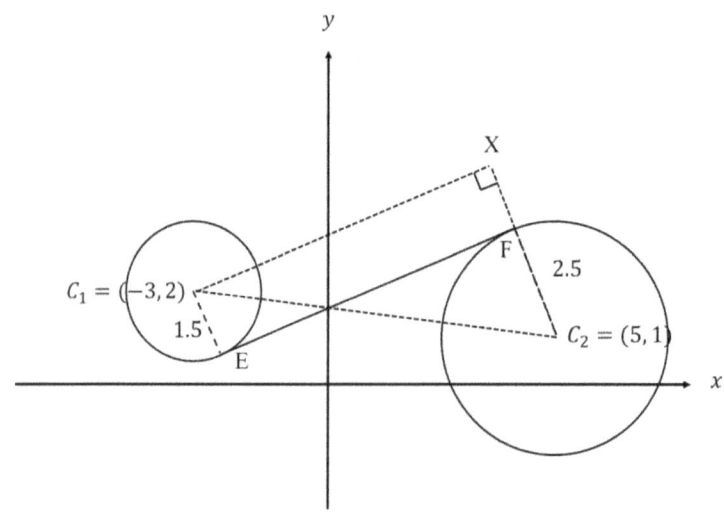

On the diagram it is clear that $C_1X = EF$ and $FX = C_1E = 1.5$. Also,

$$C_1C_2 = \sqrt{(1-2)^2 + (5-(-3))^2} = \sqrt{1+64} = \sqrt{65}$$

Hence, using Pythagoras' theorem:

$$(C_1X)^2 = (C_1C_2)^2 - (C_2X)^2 = 65 - 16 = 49$$

$$C_1X = EF = CD = 7$$

Question 23

Let H be the actual distance of the ring below the observer, then the apparent depth of the ring is $H - h$:

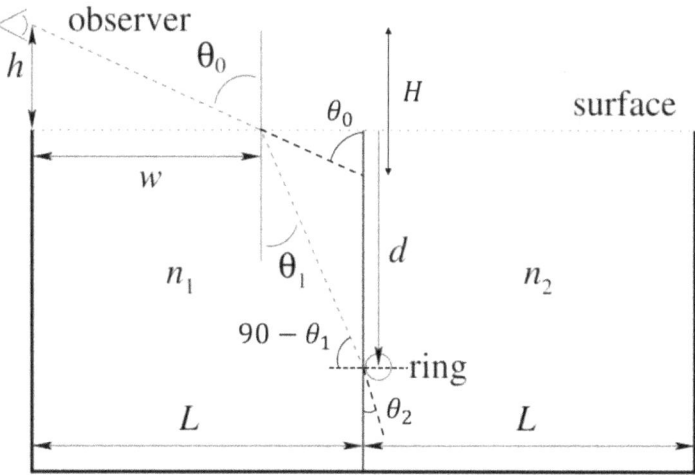

The ring will appear to stop falling at the point where total internal reflection occurs at the interface between the left and right pools. This will occur when $\theta_2 = 90°$. Hence,

$$n_1 \sin(90 - \theta_1) = n_2 \sin 90$$

$$n_1 \cos\theta_1 = n_2 \quad (1)$$

Now consider the first interface, between the air and the left pool:

$$\sin\theta_0 = n_1 \sin\theta_1 \quad (2)$$

$(1)^2 + (2)^2$:

$$n_1^2(\sin^2\theta_1 + \cos^2\theta_1) = n_2^2 + \sin^2\theta_0$$

$$\sin^2\theta_0 = n_1^2 - n_2^2 \quad (3)$$

Now consider the geometry of the above diagram:

$$\sin\theta_0 = \frac{L}{\sqrt{L^2 + H^2}}$$

$$\sin^2\theta_0 = \frac{L^2}{L^2 + H^2} \quad (4)$$

Set (3) equal to (4):

$$n_1^2 - n_2^2 = \frac{L^2}{L^2 + H^2}$$

$$H^2(n_1^2 - n_2^2) + L^2(n_1^2 - n_2^2) = L^2$$

$$H^2 = \frac{L^2(1 - n_1^2 + n_2^2)}{n_1^2 - n_2^2}$$

The apparent depth is therefore given by

$$H - h = L\sqrt{\frac{1 - n_1^2 + n_2^2}{n_1^2 - n_2^2}} - h$$

END OF PAPER

2018

Question 1: C

Each term is the sum of the previous two terms, in the same manner as the Fibonacci sequence. The next term is therefore $14 + 23 = \mathbf{37}$.

Question 2: E

All trajectories are valid except for 3, as it is a circle that is centred on $(1, 0)$, not the star.

Question 3: E

Options A-D all have units equivalent to those of force:

A: $F = qE$

B: $F = BIL$

C: $F = ma$

D: $F = \frac{Work}{Distance}$

Option E does not have units of force and is therefore the odd one out.

PAT PAST PAPER SOLUTIONS — 2018

Question 4: C

Calculate the probability of each option:

$$P(A) = \left(\frac{2}{3}\right)^3 = \frac{8}{27} \text{ (RRR)}$$

$$P(B) = \left(\frac{1}{3}\right)^3 = \frac{1}{27} \text{ (LLL)}$$

$$P(C) = 3 \times \frac{1}{3} \times \left(\frac{2}{3}\right)^2 = \frac{4}{9} \text{ (RRL, RLR, LRR)}$$

$$P(D) = 3 \times \left(\frac{1}{3}\right)^2 \times \frac{2}{3} = \frac{2}{9} \text{ (LLR, LRL, RLL)}$$

Option C is therefore the most likely combination.

Question 5: C

The number of cups of tea drunk by the person is given by

$$1 + \alpha + \alpha^2 + \alpha^3 + \cdots$$

This is a geometric series with $a = 1$ and $r = \alpha$. As the sum to infinity of the series is 3,

$$S_\infty = \frac{a}{1-r} = 3$$

$$\frac{1}{1-\alpha} = 3$$

$$3 - 3\alpha = 1$$

$$\alpha = \frac{2}{3}$$

Question 6: B

If the centre is held fixed, then consider a stationary wave of length $l = \frac{L}{2}$, where both ends are fixed. The longest wavelength occurs when $\lambda = 2l$ and subsequent harmonics occur at $\lambda_m = \frac{2l}{m}$, where m is a positive integer. Since $L = 2l$,

$$\lambda_m = \frac{L}{m}$$

Question 7: A

Since energy is conserved, the work done by the brakes must be equal to the kinetic energy lost by the car. Hence,

$$F \times d = \frac{1}{2} m u^2$$

$$F = \frac{m u^2}{2d}$$

Since the braking force acts in the opposite direction to the car's motion, it is negative:

$$F = \frac{-m u^2}{2d}$$

Question 8: A

Expand the function and differentiate:

$$y = x^2 - 2x - 3$$

$$\frac{dy}{dx} = 2x - 2$$

Since $\frac{dy}{dx} = 0$ at the minimum,

$$2x - 2 = 0$$

$$x = 1$$

Question 9: B

The gradient of the line $y = 2x - 2$ is 2, so the gradient of the perpendicular line is therefore $-\frac{1}{2}$. To find the point of intersection, substitute $x = 1$ into the original equation:

$$y = 2(1) - 2 = 0$$

Hence,

$$y - y_1 = m(x - x_1)$$

$$y - 0 = -\frac{1}{2}(x - 1)$$

$$y = -\frac{1}{2}x + \frac{1}{2}$$

Question 10: E

Substitute in values to find factors:

$$(1)^3 - (1)^2 - (1) + 1 = 0$$

$$\therefore (x - 1) \text{ is a factor}$$

$$x^3 - x^2 - x + 1 = (x - 1)(x^2 - 1)$$

$$= (x - 1)(x - 1)(x + 1)$$

The graph of $y = x^3 - x^2 - x + 1$ therefore has a root at $x = -1$ and a repeated root at $x = 1$:

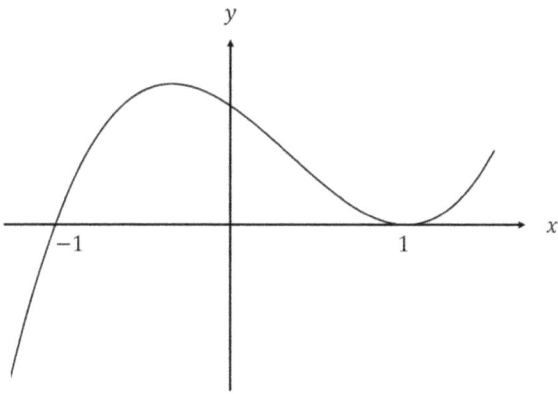

Hence, the inequality is satisfied for $x \geq -1$.

Question 11: C

The weight of the roof is

$$50 \text{ m} \times 100 \text{ m} \times 100 \text{ kgm}^{-2} \times 10 \text{ Nkg}^{-1} = 5 \times 10^6 \text{ N}$$

The cross-sectional area of the walls is approximately equal to

$$50 \times 0.1 \times 2 + 100 \times 0.1 \times 2 = 30 \text{ m}^2 = 30 \times 10^6 \text{ mm}^2$$

The stress experienced by the walls is therefore

$$\frac{5 \times 10^6}{30 \times 10^6} = 0.17 \text{ Nmm}^{-2}$$

Hence, **any of the materials could be used**.

Question 12: C

When light enters a medium with a greater refractive index, it bends towards the normal. Hence, after the ray has traversed an infinite number of plates, the light will have completely bent towards the normal and so the angle of refraction will be **zero**.

Question 13:

As stated in the question, capacitors in parallel have total capacitance given by $C_P = C_1 + C_2 + \cdots$, whilst capacitors in series have total capacitance given by $\frac{1}{C_S} = \frac{1}{C_1} + \frac{1}{C_2} + \cdots$.

On the top row there are two capacitors in series:

$$\frac{1}{C_{top}} = \frac{1}{C} + \frac{1}{C}$$

$$C_{top} = \frac{C}{2}$$

On the middle row there are two capacitors in parallel, connected in series to another capacitor:

$$\frac{1}{C_{middle}} = \frac{1}{C} + \frac{1}{2C} = \frac{3}{2C}$$

$$C_{middle} = \frac{2C}{3}$$

On the bottom row there are three capacitors in parallel: $C_{bottom} = 3C$

$$C_{tot} = C_{top} + C_{middle} + C_{bottom} = \frac{C}{2} + \frac{2C}{3} + 3C = \frac{3C + 4C + 18C}{6}$$

$$C_{tot} = \frac{25C}{6}$$

Question 14:

Use the following log identity:

$$\log_b(a) = \frac{\log_c(a)}{\log_c(b)}$$

Hence,

$$\log_x 25 = \frac{\log_5 25}{\log_5 x} = \log_5(x)$$

$$(\log_5(x))^2 = \log_5 25 = 2$$

$$\log_5 x = \pm\sqrt{2}$$

$$x = 5^{\pm\sqrt{2}}$$

Question 15:

a)

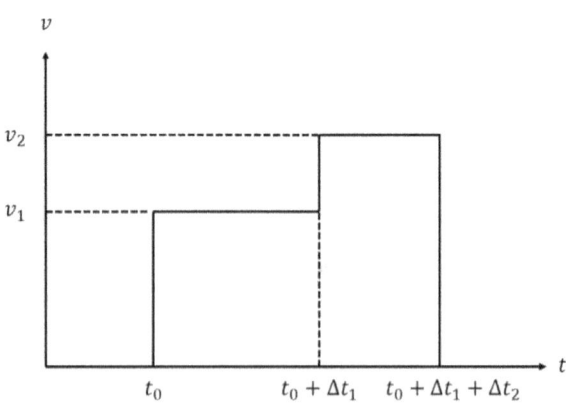

b) The average speed is equal to the total distance travelled divided by the total time. Since the distance travelled is equal to the area under the graph,

$$\langle v \rangle_t = \frac{v_1 \Delta t_1 + v_2 \Delta t_2}{\Delta t_1 + \Delta t_2} = \frac{1 \times 2 + 2 \times 1}{2 + 1} = \frac{4}{3} \text{ ms}^{-1}$$

c)

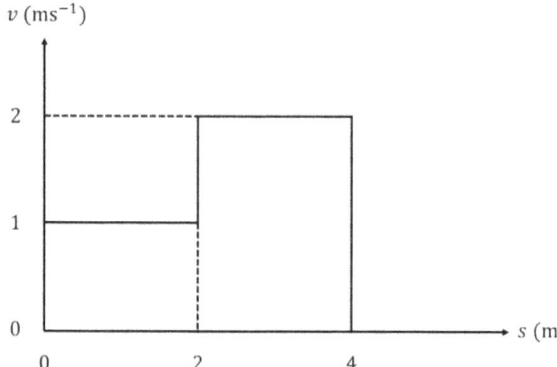

d) Use the same approach as for the time weighted average, replacing change in time with change in distance:

$$\langle v \rangle_s = \frac{v_1 \Delta s_1 + v_2 \Delta s_2}{\Delta s_1 + \Delta s_2} = \frac{1 \times 2 + 2 \times 2}{2 + 2} = \frac{3}{2} \text{ ms}^{-1}$$

e) This means that $\langle v \rangle_c = \langle v \rangle_t$.

f) Integrate with respect to time to find the distance travelled, then divide by the total time.

Question 16:

First, calculate the area of the hexagon by breaking it up into triangles:

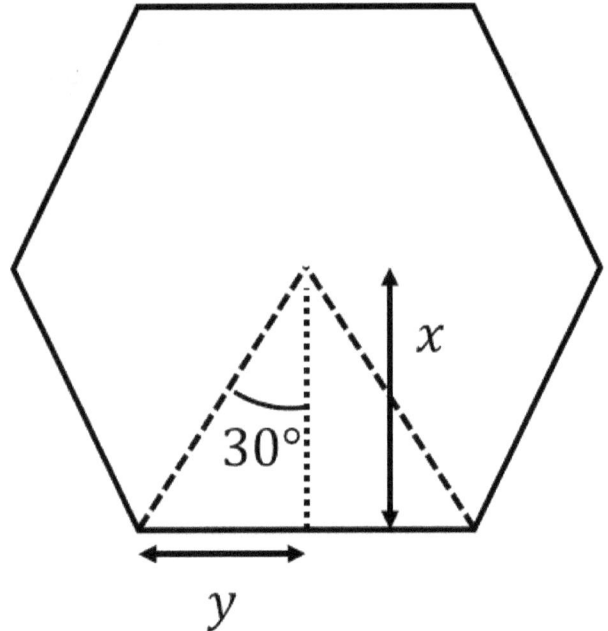

Considering the right-angled triangle formed,

$$\tan 30 = \frac{y}{x}$$

$$y = \frac{x}{\sqrt{3}}$$

The area of the triangle is therefore

$$A_t = \frac{1}{2} \times 2y \times x = \frac{1}{2} \times \frac{2x}{\sqrt{3}} \times x = \frac{x^2}{\sqrt{3}}$$

Hence, the area of the hexagon is

$$A_h = \frac{6x^2}{\sqrt{3}} = 2\sqrt{3}x^2$$

Given that the area of the circle is $A_c = \pi r^2$,

$$A_h = 4A_c$$

$$2\sqrt{3}x^2 = 4\pi r^2$$

$$x = r\left(\frac{2\pi}{\sqrt{3}}\right)^{\frac{1}{2}}$$

Question 17:

First, evaluate the exact integral:

$$\int_0^{0.1} (1+x)^9 dx = \left[\frac{(1+x)^{10}}{10}\right]_0^{0.1} = \frac{1}{10}(1.1^{10} - 1) = 0.1594$$

Expanding the expression inside the integral first and then integrating gives

$$\int_0^{0.1} (1+x)^9 dx \approx \int_0^{0.1} \left[1 + 9x + \frac{9(8)x^2}{2} + \frac{9(8)(7)x^3}{6} + \cdots\right] dx$$

$$= \left[x + \frac{9x^2}{2} + 12x^3 + 21x^4 + \cdots\right]_0^{0.1}$$

$$= 0.1 + 0.045 + 0.012 + 0.0021 + \cdots$$

The zero-order expansion gives 0.1. The first-order expansion gives $0.1 + 0.045 = 0.145$, which is less than 10% error. Hence, a **first-order expansion** is required.

Question 18:

a) A free body diagram of the left sphere is shown below:

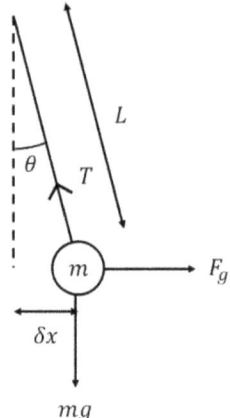

Consider vertical equilibrium: $T \cos \theta = mg$ (1)

Consider horizontal equilibrium: $T \sin \theta = F_g$ (2)

(2) ÷ (1):

$$\frac{T \sin \theta}{T \cos \theta} = \frac{F_g}{mg}$$

$$\tan \theta = \frac{F_g}{mg}$$

$$\tan \theta = \left(\frac{1}{mg}\right) \frac{Gmm}{(x - 2\delta x)^2}$$

$$\tan \theta = \frac{Gm}{g(x^2 - 4x\delta x + 4(\delta x)^2)}$$

Since $\delta x \ll x$,

$$\tan\theta = \frac{Gm}{g(x^2 - 4x\delta x)}$$

Considering the geometry in the question,

$$\sin\theta = \frac{\delta x}{L}$$

As θ is very small,

$$\tan\theta \approx \sin\theta$$

$$\tan\theta \approx \frac{\delta x}{L}$$

$$\frac{\delta x}{L} \approx \frac{Gm}{g(x^2 - 4x\delta x)}$$

$$g\delta x(x^2 - 4x\delta x) = GmL$$

$$4gx(\delta x)^2 - gx^2\delta x + GmL = 0$$

This is a quadratic in δx, so use the quadratic formula:

$$\delta x = \frac{gx^2 \pm \sqrt{(-gx^2)^2 - 4(4gx)(GmL)}}{8gx}$$

$$\delta x = \frac{gx^2}{8gx} \pm \sqrt{\frac{g^2x^4 - 16gxGmL}{64g^2x^2}}$$

$$\delta x = \frac{x}{8} \pm \sqrt{\frac{x^2}{64} - \frac{GmL}{4gx}} \qquad \delta x = \frac{x}{8} \pm \sqrt{\left(\frac{x}{8}\right)^2 - \frac{LmG}{4gx}}$$

As $m \to 0$, $\delta x \to 0$ as there would be no gravitational force. Therefore, only the negative square root is included in the solution:

$$\delta x = \frac{x}{8} - \sqrt{\left(\frac{x}{8}\right)^2 - \frac{LmG}{4gx}}$$

b) The gravitational force must be equal to the force due to the spheres being charged:

$$\frac{Gm^2}{x^2} = \frac{kQ^2}{x^2}$$

$$Q = m\sqrt{\frac{G}{k}}$$

Question 19:

a) Power and voltage are related using the equation $P = \frac{V^2}{R}$. Hence,

$$R_A = \frac{100^2}{100} = 100 \, \Omega \text{ and } R_B = \frac{100^2}{20} = 500 \, \Omega$$

Lamp B has the greater resistance and will therefore be brighter. To find the brightness ratio, use the equation $P = I^2 R$:

$$\frac{P_A}{P_B} = \frac{I_A^2 R_A}{I_B^2 R_B}$$

Since the lamps are in series, $I_A = I_B$:

$$\frac{P_A}{P_B} = \frac{R_A}{R_B} = \frac{1}{5}$$

b) If the lamps were wired in parallel, they would then have the same voltage across them, so use the equation $P = \frac{V^2}{R}$:

$$\frac{P_A}{P_B} = \frac{V^2/R_A}{V^2/R_B} = \frac{R_B}{R_A} = 5$$

Hence, lamp A is now brighter.

Question 20:

a) All the four planes have either 'all odd' or 'all even' (given the assumption that 0 is even). Therefore, the lattice is **face centred cubic**.

b) Rearranging for a gives: $a = d\sqrt{h^2 + k^2 + l^2}$

For each of the values given:

d (mm)	Plane	a (mm²)
0.224	(111)	0.388
0.195	(200)	0.390
0.137	(220)	0.387
0.117	(311)	0.388

Find the mean value for the best estimate:

$$\bar{a} = \frac{0.388 + 0.390 + 0.387 + 0.388}{4} = \mathbf{0.388}$$

c) Initially,
$$V = L^3 = (Na)^3$$

Let x be the length of the unknown sides. After deformation, the volume is given by

$$V = x^2 L' = x^2 \left(\frac{2}{3} Na\right)$$

Since the volume remains constant,

$$\frac{2}{3} x^2 Na = (Na)^3$$

$$x^2 = \frac{3N^2 a^2}{2}$$

$$x = \sqrt{\frac{3}{2}} Na$$

Question 21:

a) The minimal force is equal to the centripetal force:
$$F(r) = mr\omega^2$$

b) The work done is equal to the integral of the force with respect to distance, but with a negative sign as the force acts in the opposite direction to positive r:

$$W = \int F(r)\, dr = -\int_{r_0}^{0} mr\omega^2 \, dr$$

c) The child's work is converted into (rotational) **kinetic energy**, and as such the angular speed will increase as the child approaches the centre.

d)

$$J = I\omega = (mr^2 + I_p)\omega$$

$$\omega(r) = \frac{J}{mr^2 + I_p}$$

e) Substitute the expression for part (d) into the integral in part (b):

$$W = -\int_{r_0}^{0} mr\omega^2 dr = -\int_{r_0}^{0} mr\left(\frac{J}{mr^2 + I_p}\right)^2 dr$$

$$W = -mJ^2 \int_{r_0}^{0} \frac{r}{m^2\left(r^2 + \frac{I_p}{m}\right)^2} dr = -\frac{J^2}{m}\int_{r_0}^{0} \frac{r}{\left(r^2 + \frac{I_p}{m}\right)^2} dr$$

Using the integral given in the question,

$$W = -\frac{J^2}{m}\left[\frac{-1}{2\left(r^2 + \frac{I_p}{m}\right)}\right]_{r_0}^{0} = \frac{J^2}{2m}\left(\frac{1}{(I_p/m)} - \frac{1}{r_0^2 + \frac{I_p}{m}}\right)$$

$$W = \frac{J^2}{2m}\left(\frac{m}{I_p} - \frac{m}{I_p + r_0^2}\right) = \frac{J^2}{2}\left(\frac{1}{I_p} - \frac{1}{I_p + mr_0^2}\right)$$

Question 22:

Firstly, rearrange the equation of the circle into the standard form:

$$x^2 + y^2 - 8x + 4y + 4 = 0$$

$$(x-4)^2 - 16 + (y+2)^2 - 4 + 4 = 0$$

$$(x-4)^2 + (y+2)^2 = 4^2$$

This is therefore a circle with centre $(4, -2)$ and radius $r = 4$:

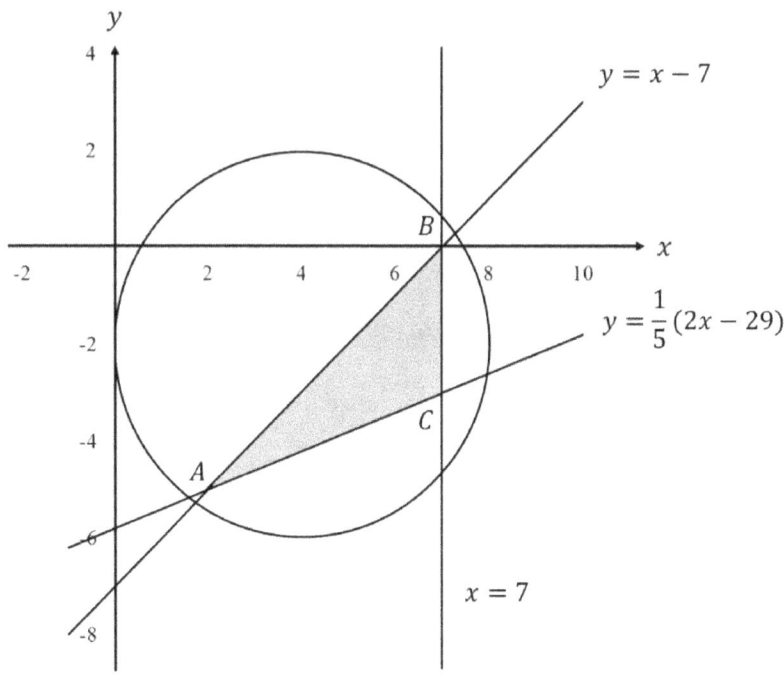

The coordinates A, B and C can be found by finding the intersections between the relevant lines. At A,

$$x - 7 = \frac{1}{5}(2x - 29)$$

$$5x - 35 = 2x - 29$$

$$3x = 6$$

$$x = 2$$

$$A = (2, -5)$$

B and C can be found by substituting $x = 7$ into the equations of the two lines:

$$B = (7, 0), C = (7, -3)$$

The area of the shaded triangle is then given by

$$A_t = \frac{1}{2} \times base \times height$$

The base is equal to the horizontal distance between A and C, whilst the height is equal to BC.

$$A_t = \frac{1}{2} \times 5 \times 3 = \frac{15}{2}$$

The area of the circle is given by

$$A_c = \pi r^2 = \pi(4^2) = 16\pi$$

Hence, the area inside the circle but outside the triangle is

$$A = A_c - A_t = 16\pi - \frac{15}{2}$$

Question 23:

$$f(x) = \frac{\sqrt{x^2 - 2}}{\ln(3x + 10)}$$

In order for this to be real: $x^2 - 2 \geq 0$ so $x \geq \sqrt{2}$ or $x \leq -\sqrt{2}$.

In order for the denominator to be defined (a logarithm is undefined for any number ≤ 0): $3x + 10 > 0$ so $x > -\frac{10}{3}$.

In order for the function to be finite, the denominator must not be zero:

$$\ln(3x + 10) \neq 0$$

$$3x + 10 \neq 1$$

$$x \neq -3$$

Combining these gives:

$$-\frac{10}{3} < x \leq -\sqrt{2}, \qquad x \geq \sqrt{2}, \qquad x \neq -3$$

END OF PAPER

2019

Question 1: D

By inspection, this is a geometric progression as each term is multiplied by a common ratio: $r = -\frac{1}{3}$. The next number is $-12 \times -\frac{1}{3} = 4$.

Question 2: A

The two equations can be rearranged into standard simultaneous equations without logs. Consider the first equation:

$$\log x + 2\log y = \log 32$$

$$\log x + \log(y^2) = \log 32$$

$$\log(xy^2) = \log 32$$

$$xy^2 = 32$$

Now consider the second equation:

$$\log x - \log y = -\log 2$$

$$\log\left(\frac{x}{y}\right) = \log\left(\frac{1}{2}\right)$$

$$\frac{x}{y} = \frac{1}{2}$$

$$y = 2x$$

Substituting $y = 2x$ into $xy^2 = 32$ and rearranging gives the solution:

$$x \times (2x)^2 = 32$$

$$x = 2, y = 4$$

Question 3: C

For potential energy due to gravity, $V(r) \propto \frac{1}{r}$ and so $n = -1$.

Therefore $2 \langle T_{tot} \rangle = - \langle V_{tot} \rangle$. Since the particles only interact via gravity, total energy is calculated as

$$\langle E_{tot} \rangle = \langle V_{tot} \rangle + \langle T_{tot} \rangle$$

$$\langle E_{tot} \rangle = \langle V_{tot} \rangle - \frac{1}{2} \langle V_{tot} \rangle$$

$$\langle E_{tot} \rangle = \frac{\langle V_{tot} \rangle}{2}$$

Question 4: A

The mass of the Earth is given by $M = \frac{4}{3} \pi R^3 \rho$, where ρ is its density.

$$g_{Earth} = \frac{4}{3} \frac{\rho \pi G R^3}{R^2} = \frac{4}{3} \rho \pi G R$$

The acceleration due to gravity, g_{planet}, on the planet in the different universe is

$$g_{planet} = \frac{4}{3} \rho' \pi G' R' = \frac{4}{3} (2\rho) \pi (2G) \left(\frac{R}{2} \right) = 2 \times \frac{4}{3} \rho \pi G R$$

$$\frac{g_{planet}}{g_{Earth}} = 2$$

Question 5: A

For this question, the trigonometric identity $\tan^2 \theta + 1 = \sec^2 \theta$ is required. Substituting this into the equation in the question gives

$$(1 + \tan^2 \theta) + \alpha \tan \theta = 0$$

This is now a quadratic of the form $a \tan^2 \theta + b \tan \theta + c = 0$, for which real solutions are only obtained when $b^2 - 4ac \geq 0$.

$$\alpha^2 - 4 \geq 0$$

$$\alpha \leq -2 \text{ or } \alpha \geq 2$$

Question 6: A

Consider the probability tree for the different outcomes of drawing two balls from the bag, as shown below. It is important to note that, since the balls aren't replaced, there will only be $b + r - 1$ balls remaining after the first ball is drawn.

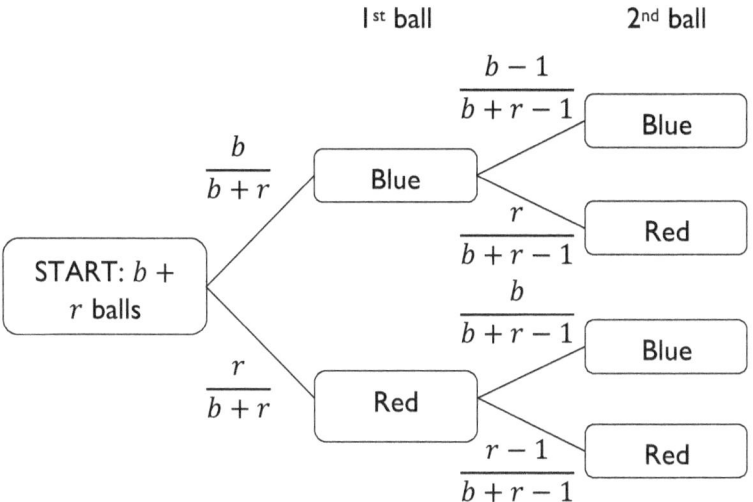

There are two possible paths through the tree that result in two different colours: blue then red or red then blue. The probability of a path occurring is found by multiplying the probability of the 1st and 2nd balls being drawn, as these events are independent. The probabilities for the two different paths can then be summed to find the overall probability of picking two different colours:

$$\frac{b}{b+r} \times \frac{r}{b+r-1} + \frac{r}{b+r} \times \frac{b}{b+r-1} = \frac{2br}{(b+r)(b+r-1)}$$

Question 7: E

Any finger can either be stretched out or curled up, giving two possible states. To be able to represent the most integers, the fingers can be considered binary digits and so one finger can represent two integers, two fingers together can represent four integers and so on. The number of integers that can be represented by n fingers is 2^n, therefore 10 fingers can represent $2^{10} = \mathbf{1024}$ different integers.

Question 8: A

The integral of an odd function with limits that are symmetric about the origin is always zero. For a function $f(x)$, if $f(-x) = -f(x)$ then the function is odd, and the integral is zero. If $f(-x) = f(x)$, the function is even. Evaluating each of the four functions in this way reveals that the functions in I_1 and I_4 are odd and hence these integrals are zero. The functions in I_2 and I_3 are even and by inspection they are always positive, so their integrals must be non-zero.

Question 9: D

The magnetic field points circumferentially around the wire according to the right-hand rule, such that if the current is flowing into the page, the magnetic field is in a clockwise direction and if the current flows out of the page, the field is in an anticlockwise direction. $B = \frac{\alpha I}{r}$ so, at an equidistant point where $r = \frac{D}{2}$ for both wires, the magnitude of the current in the second wire must also be I for B to double. However, as the magnetic fields must be in the same direction to sum together, the current in the second wire must be in the opposite direction (as shown in the figure below) and therefore $I_2 = -I$.

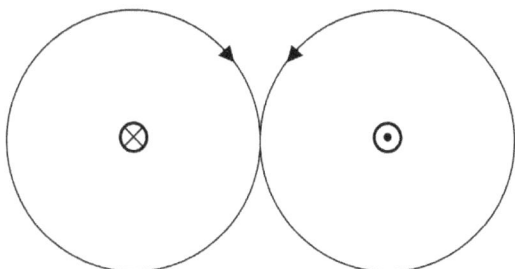

Question 10: E

The phase of the Earth as seen from the Moon is the opposite to the phase of the Moon as seen from the Earth. Therefore, when a Full Moon is seen from Earth, a **"New Earth"** is seen from the Moon.

Question 11: C

The total resistance of resistors in series is $R_s = R_1 + R_2$ and the total resistance of resistors in parallel is $\frac{1}{R_p} = \frac{1}{R_1} + \frac{1}{R_2}$, or $R_p = \frac{R_1 R_2}{R_1 + R_2}$. Using these formulae, the resistance of path A is

$$R_A = R + \frac{R \times R}{R + R} = \frac{3}{2}R$$

The resistance of path B is similarly calculated as $R_B = 2R$. The total resistance, R_T, achieved when both switches are closed is

$$R_T = \frac{R_A \times R_B}{R_A + R_B} = \frac{\frac{3}{2}R \times 2R}{\frac{3}{2}R + 2R} = \frac{6}{7}R$$

The maximum brightness occurs at the lowest resistance and the minimum brightness at highest resistance. The minimum to maximum brightness therefore occurs in the order: **B closed, A closed, both closed**.

Question 12: B

When a standing wave is set up in a pipe with one end open and the other closed, there will be an antinode at the open end of the pipe and a node at the closed end. At the fundamental (minimum) frequency, the wave will be set up as shown in the diagram below, where $L = \frac{\lambda}{4}$. Substituting this into $v = f\lambda$ at $f = f_{min}$ gives

$$L = \frac{v}{4f_{min}}$$

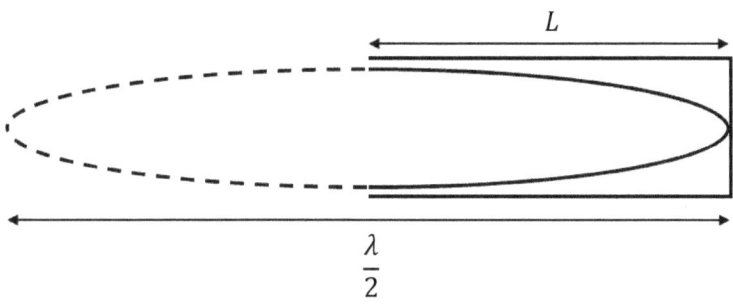

Question 13:

a)

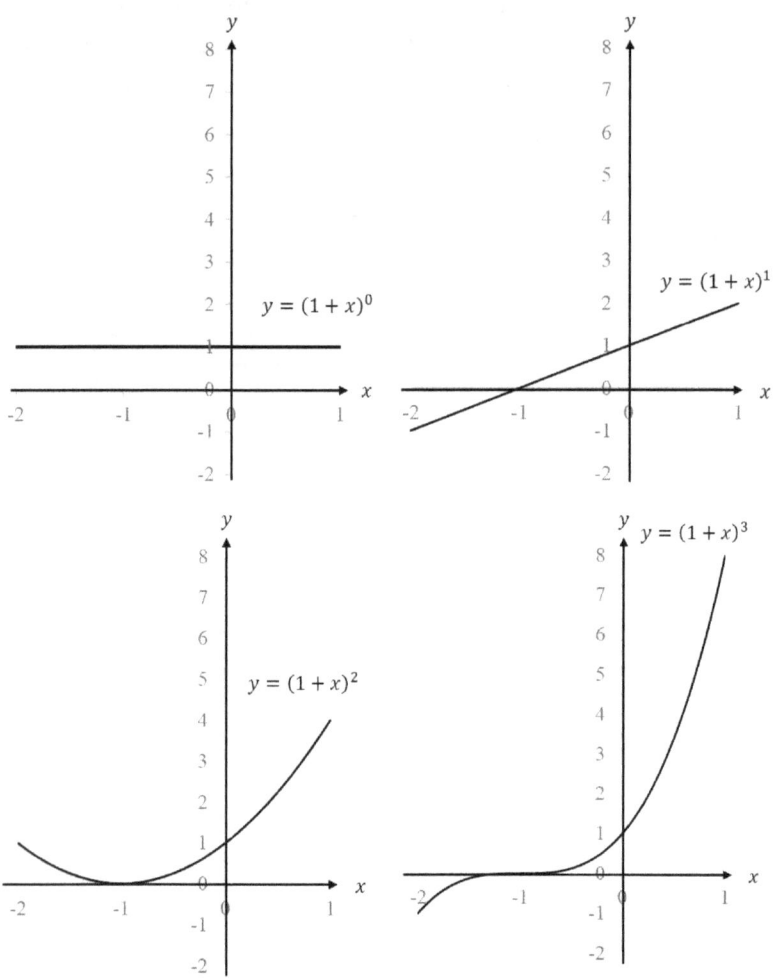

The point $(0, 1)$ is common to all graphs.

b) All graphs for which $n > 1$ have a single turning point at $(-1, 0)$. They also have an increasing, positive gradient for all $x > -1$.

Question 14:

a) At time $t = t_{1/2}$,

$$\frac{N_A(t_{1/2})}{N_{A0}} = e^{-\lambda t_{1/2}} = \frac{1}{2}$$

$$-\lambda t_{1/2} = \ln\frac{1}{2}$$

$$\lambda t_{1/2} = \ln 2$$

$$\lambda = \frac{\ln 2}{t_{1/2}}$$

b) Since isotope A decays to isotope B, the increase in the number of B atoms is equal to the decrease in the number of A atoms.

$$N_B(t) = N_{B0} + (N_{A0} - N_A(t))$$

$$N_B(t) = N_{B0} + N_{A0}(1 - e^{-\lambda t})$$

c) The initial condition is $N_{A0} = xN_{B0}$. Let T be the time at which the ratio is reversed:

$$N_B(T) = xN_A(T)$$

Substitute the expression for N_B from part (b) into the equation above:

$$N_{B0} + N_{A0}(1 - e^{-\lambda T}) = xN_{A0}e^{-\lambda T}$$

Substitute in the initial condition:

$$N_{B0} + xN_{B0}(1 - e^{-\lambda T}) = x^2 N_{B0} e^{-\lambda T}$$

$$1 + x(1 - e^{-\lambda T}) = x^2 e^{-\lambda T}$$

$$e^{\lambda T} + x(e^{\lambda T} - 1) = x^2$$

$$e^{\lambda T}(1 + x) = x^2 + x$$

$$e^{\lambda T} = \frac{x(x+1)}{x+1} = x$$

$$\lambda T = \ln x$$

$$T = \frac{\ln x}{\lambda}$$

Question 15:

a)

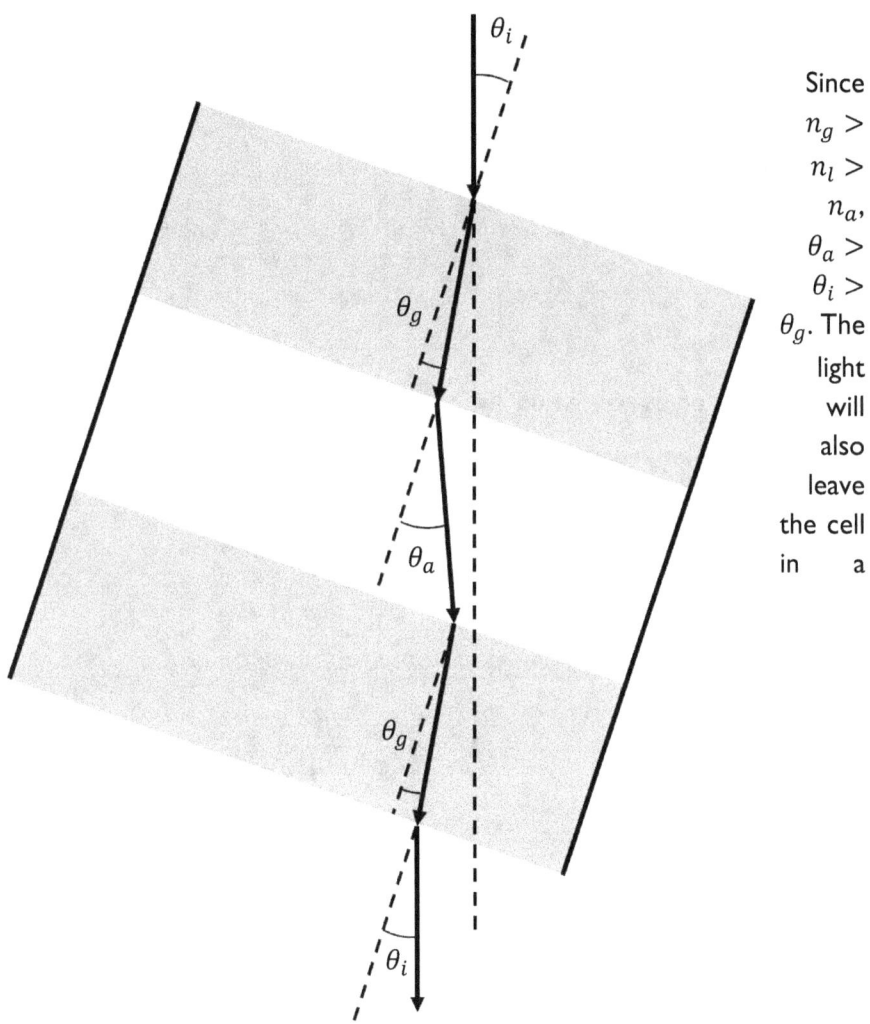

Since $n_g > n_l > n_a$, $\theta_a > \theta_i > \theta_g$. The light will also leave the cell in a direction parallel to its initial incidence.

b) As θ_i increases from zero, the observed beam of light at the exit will move sideways. It will continue moving sideways until total internal reflection occurs at the glass-air interface.

$$n_l \sin \theta_i = n_g \sin \theta_g = n_a \sin 90$$

$$n_l = \frac{n_a}{\sin \theta_i}$$

c) By using a gas with a higher refractive index than air, θ_i will increase at total internal reflection and so can be measured more accurately,

Question 16:

a) The energy of a photon is given by $E = hf$. By substituting $f = \frac{c}{\lambda}$,

$$E = \frac{hc}{\lambda}$$

b) The energy released by the transition is $E = -hcR\left(\frac{1}{p^2} - \frac{1}{q^2}\right)$. The equation in part (a) can then be substituted in:

$$\frac{hc}{\lambda} = -hcR\left(\frac{1}{p^2} - \frac{1}{q^2}\right)$$

$$\frac{1}{\lambda} = R\left(\frac{1}{q^2} - \frac{1}{p^2}\right) = R\left(\frac{p^2 - q^2}{p^2 q^2}\right)$$

$$\lambda = \frac{1}{R}\left(\frac{p^2 q^2}{p^2 - q^2}\right)$$

c) Consider the wavelength of light emitted when transitioning from level q to $p = q + 1$:

$$\lambda = \frac{1}{R}\left(\frac{(q+1)^2 q^2}{(q+1)^2 - q^2}\right)$$

$$\lambda = \frac{q^2(q+1)^2}{R(2q+1)}$$

Create a table of values for $1 \leq q < 6$:

q	λ_{q+1} (nm)
1	121.50
2	656.11
3	1874.6
4	4050.1
5	7455.8

Comparing these calculations to the wavelengths given for $(q + 1)$ in the question shows that Set-A has $q = 1$, Set-B has $q = 4$ and Set-C has $q = 5$.

Question 17:

a)

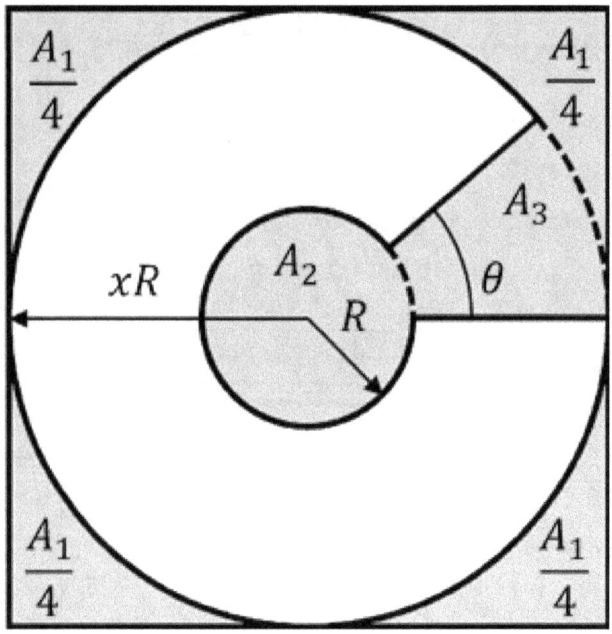

$$A_s = (2xR)^2 = 4x^2R^2$$

Based on the areas shown in the figure above,

$$A_1 = A_s - \pi(xR)^2 = x^2R^2(4 - \pi)$$

$$A_2 = \pi R^2$$

$$A_3 = \frac{\theta}{2\pi}\pi((xR)^2 - R^2) = \frac{\theta R^2}{2}(x^2 - 1)$$

$$A_g = A_1 + A_2 + A_3 = R^2\left(x^2(4 - \pi) + \pi + \frac{\theta}{2}(x^2 - 1)\right)$$

As stated in the question,

$$A_g = fA_s$$

$$R^2\left(x^2(4-\pi) + \pi + \frac{\theta}{2}(x^2-1)\right) = 4fx^2R^2$$

$$4x^2 + \pi(1-x^2) + \frac{\theta}{2}(x^2-1) = 4fx^2$$

$$\theta = \frac{2}{x^2-1}(4fx^2 - 4x^2 + \pi(x^2-1)) = 2\pi + \frac{2(4fx^2 - 4x^2)}{x^2-1}$$

$$\theta = 2\pi - \frac{8(1-f)x^2}{x^2-1} \equiv B - \frac{C(f)x^2}{x^2-1}$$

where $B = 2\pi$ and $C(f) = 8(1-f)$.

b) Substitute $x = 3$ and $f = \frac{1}{2}$ into the previous equation:

$$\theta = 2\pi - \frac{8\left(1-\frac{1}{2}\right) \times 3^2}{3^2 - 1}$$

$$\theta = 2\pi - \frac{9}{2}$$

$$\boldsymbol{\theta = 1.7832 \text{ rads (5sf)}}$$

Question 18:

$$\frac{e^x + 9}{e^{-x} + 5} = 2$$

$$e^x + 9 = 2e^{-x} + 10$$

$$e^x - 1 - 2e^{-x} = 0$$

$$e^{2x} - e^x - 2 = 0$$

Since $e^{2x} = (e^x)^2$, this is a quadratic in e^x which can be solved using the quadratic formula:

$$e^x = \frac{1 \pm \sqrt{(-1)^2 - 4 \times (-2)}}{2}$$

$$e^x = \frac{1 \pm 3}{2}$$

$$e^x = 2 \text{ or } -1$$

Since $e^x > 0$ for all x, the only solution is $e^x = 2$. Hence,

$$x = \ln 2$$

Question 19:

a) Conservation of mass:

$$m_0 = m_1 + m_2 + m_3 + m_4 = 10 \text{ g}$$

Conservation of momentum (vertically):

$$m_0 v_0 = m_1 v_1 + m_4 v_4$$

$$10 \times 2 = 1 \times v_1 + 4 \times 1$$

$$v_1 = 16 \text{ ms}^{-1} \text{ (upwards)}$$

Conservation of momentum (horizontally):

$$m_2 v_2 + m_3 v_3 = 0$$

$$2v_2 + 3v_3 = 0$$

$$v_2 = -\frac{3}{2} v_3$$

Conservation of energy:

$$\frac{1}{2} m_0 v_0^2 + E_{exp} = \frac{1}{2} m_1 v_1^2 + \frac{1}{2} m_2 v_2^2 + \frac{1}{2} m_3 v_3^2 + \frac{1}{2} m_4 v_4^2$$

$$m_0 v_0^2 + 2 E_{exp} = m_1 v_1^2 + m_2 v_2^2 + m_3 v_3^2 + m_4 v_4^2$$

Multiplying E_{exp} by 10^3 (since all masses are in grams) and substituting in values gives

$$10 \times 2^2 + 2 \times 1 \times 10^3 = 1 \times 16^2 + 2 \times \left(-\frac{3}{2} v_3\right)^2 + 3 \times v_3^2 + 4 \times 1^2$$

$$2040 = 260 + \frac{15}{2} v_3^2$$

$$v_3 = 15.4 \text{ ms}^{-1}, \quad v_2 = 23.1 \text{ ms}^{-1} \text{ (in the opposite direction to } v_3\text{)}$$

b) The maximum speed would be achieved by m_1 travelling upwards if all the other pieces travel directly downwards. As m_0 initially has only vertical momentum upwards, the movement of all three other pieces downwards further propels m_1 upwards due to conservation of momentum. m_1 is chosen as it is the lightest piece and so will travel fastest in this situation.

Question 20:

a)

$$I = I_p + I_q \cos\left(\frac{2\pi L}{\lambda}\right)$$

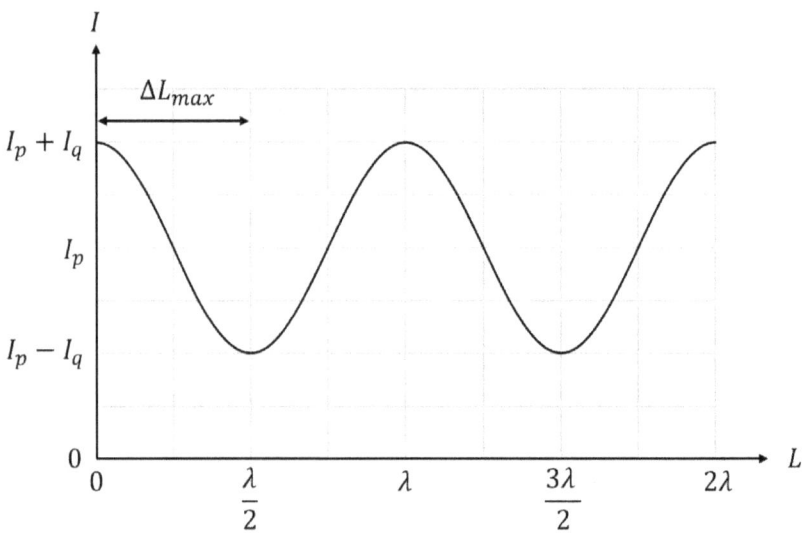

b) The biggest ΔL that can be unambiguously inferred is equal to $\frac{\lambda}{2}$. Only by increasing L from zero until the first intensity minimum can a reliable ΔL be measured.

Question 21:

a) The minimum delay, L_{min}, occurs when all n switches are turned to the lower position:

$$L_{min} = nl$$

$$l = \frac{L_{min}}{n}$$

b) For a system where the added delay at each stage, L_i, can either be turned on or off and given the objective of achieving every multiple of δL using the minimum number of switches, a binary numbering system is required. This means that the values of L_i need to be powers of 2, with $L_1 = \delta L$, $L_2 = 2\delta L$, $L_3 = 4\delta L$ and so on. The general term for L_i is therefore

$$L_i = 2^{i-1} \times \delta L$$

c) The final condition on the values of L_i is that if all switches are turned to the upper value of $l + L_i$ then the total delay is $L_{min} + \Delta L$:

$$\sum_i^n (L_i + l) = L_{min} + \Delta L$$

$$nl + \sum_i^n L_i = L_{min} + \Delta L$$

Since $L_{min} = nl$ from part (a):

$$\sum_i^n L_i = \Delta L$$

Substitute for L_i from part (b):

$$\sum_{i}^{n} 2^{i-1} \times \delta L = \Delta L$$

$$\sum_{i}^{n} 2^{i-1} = \frac{\Delta L}{\delta L}$$

This is a geometric series with first term $= 1$ and ratio $= 2$.

$$\sum_{i}^{n} 2^{i-1} = \frac{a(r^n - 1)}{r - 1} = 2^n - 1$$

$$2^n - 1 = \frac{\Delta L}{\delta L}$$

$$2^n = 1 + \frac{\Delta L}{\delta L}$$

$$n = \log_2\left(1 + \frac{\Delta L}{\delta L}\right)$$

Question 22:

The volume of a cone is $V = \frac{1}{3}\pi r^2 H$, where $r = \frac{D}{2}$. Therefore,

$$V = \frac{1}{3}\pi \left(\frac{D}{2}\right)^2 H = \frac{1}{12}\pi D^2 H$$

At any height, h, on this cone the diameter, d, will be scaled according to $d = D\frac{h}{H}$ (since the cones are similar). The volume, v, at any height is hence given by $v = \frac{1}{12}\pi \left(D\frac{h}{H}\right)^2 h$. This means that $v \propto h^3$. Halving v therefore causes h to be multiplied by $\frac{1}{\sqrt[3]{2}}$.

$$\text{Therefore at } v = \frac{V}{2}, \, \boldsymbol{h} = \frac{H}{\sqrt[3]{2}}.$$

Question 23:

The fraction of impurity removed, f, on the ith pass is $f_i = \frac{1}{n^i}$. After m passes, the total fraction of impurity removed is F:

$$F = \sum_i^m f_i$$

$$F = \sum_i^m \frac{1}{n^i}$$

When $n = 2$, F is a geometric series with first term $= \frac{1}{2}$ and ratio $= \frac{1}{2}$:

$$F = \frac{\frac{1}{2}\left(1 - \frac{1}{2^m}\right)}{1 - \frac{1}{2}}$$

$$F = 1 - \frac{1}{2^m}$$

As $m \to \infty$, $F \to 1$, so the amount of impurity remaining tends to zero. This means that the water can be made arbitrarily pure by choosing m. When $n = 3$,

$$F = \frac{\frac{1}{3}\left(1 - \frac{1}{3^m}\right)}{1 - \frac{1}{3}}$$

$$F = \frac{1}{2}\left(1 - \frac{1}{3^m}\right)$$

In this case, as $m \to \infty$, $F \to \frac{1}{2}$ and so only half of the impurity can ever be removed.

Question 24:

In this question, the diagram is slightly misleading. Note that the spring has unstretched length R_0 plus an extension of R giving a total length of $L = R_0 + R$.

a) Hooke's law states that the force in the spring is $F_s = kR$, whilst the centripetal force is $F_c = m(R + R_0)\omega^2$. At equilibrium, $F_s = F_c$.

$$m(R + R_0)\omega^2 = kR$$

$$R(k - m\omega^2) = m\omega^2 R_0$$

$$R = \frac{m\omega^2 R_0}{k - m\omega^2}$$

b) According to Hooke's Law,

$$F_{max} = kR_{max} = \frac{km\omega_c^2 R_0}{k - m\omega_c^2}$$

$$F_{max}(k - m\omega_c^2) = km\omega_c^2 R_0$$

$$\omega_c^2(kmR_0 + mF_{max}) = kF_{max}$$

$$\omega_c^2 = \frac{kF_{max}}{m(kR_0 + F_{max})}$$

$$\omega_c = \sqrt{\frac{kF_{max}}{m(kR_0 + F_{max})}}$$

c) Substitute in the values $m = 1$ kg, $R_0 = 1$ m and $k = 1$ Nm^{-1}:

$$\omega_c = \sqrt{\frac{F_{max}}{F_{max} + 1}}$$

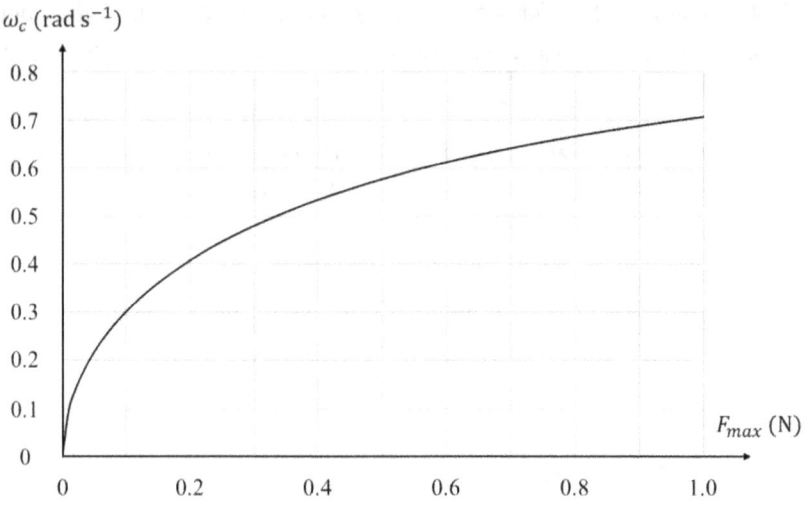

d) As ω approaches the system's natural frequency, the system will begin to resonate. The amplitude of the oscillations becomes larger and larger until the force in the spring exceeds F_{max} and the spring breaks. The natural frequency is that denoted by ω_i in the question. The formula for this frequency is

$$\omega_i = \sqrt{\frac{k}{m}}$$

END OF PAPER

Afterword

Remember that the route to a high score is your approach and practice. Don't fall into the trap that *"you can't prepare for the PAT"* – this couldn't be further from the truth. With knowledge of the test, time-saving techniques and plenty of practice you can dramatically boost your score.

Work hard, never give up and do yourself justice.

Good luck!

Acknowledgements

Thanks must go to *Samuel* for his tremendous help in putting this set of answers together.

Rohan

About Us

We currently publish over 85 titles across a range of subject areas – covering specialised admissions tests, examination techniques, personal statement guides, plus everything else you need to improve your chances of getting on to competitive courses such as medicine and law, as well as into universities such as Oxford and Cambridge.

Outside of publishing we also operate a highly successful tuition division, called UniAdmissions. This company was founded in 2013 by Dr Rohan Agarwal and Dr David Salt, both Cambridge Medical graduates with several years of tutoring experience. Since then, every year, hundreds of applicants and schools work with us on our programmes. Through the programmes we offer, we deliver expert tuition, exclusive course places, online courses, best-selling textbooks and much more.

With a team of over 1,000 Oxbridge tutors and a proven track record, UniAdmissions have quickly become the UK's number one admissions company.

Visit and engage with us at:
Website (UniAdmissions): www.uniadmissions.co.uk
Facebook: www.facebook.com/uniadmissionsuk

www.ingramcontent.com/pod-product-compliance
Lightning Source LLC
Chambersburg PA
CBHW050301010526
44108CB00040B/1964